Norma Rose.

THE STARTLING TRUTH ABOUT

* Why Margaret could never marry the first man she really loved.

* Why Robin Douglas-Home committed suicide for her.

* Margaret and Tony's chronic extramarital affairs.

* Margaret's fits of despondency and weakness for vodka.

* Her abuse of her royal allowance.

And dozens of other never-before-revealed facts about the PRINCESS WHO FELL FROM GRACE—AND INTO THE WORLD'S HEADLINES!

MARGARET, THE IMPERFECT PRINCESS

by **SUZANNE MUNSHOWER**

A BERKLEY MEDALLION BOOK
published by
BERKLEY PUBLISHING CORPORATION

for my mother and father,
whose love and encouragement
have made everything possible

Prologue

Her Royal Highness Princess Margaret of Great Britain is known the world over as a scintillating conversationalist who's in peak form when relating witty anecdotes. And there are few stories she loves to tell more than that recalling the earliest memory of her life. Margaret can clearly remember when, as little more than a babe in arms, she toppled out of her pram. The entire household staff of her parents, who were then the Duke and Duchess of York, came running fearfully to her rescue, only to discover with relief that the child was unharmed. As Margaret laughingly admits, "I must have wanted to be noticed."

She couldn't have spoken more epigrammatically of her entire forty-seven years.

As most of the world now knows, any desires to be noticed were instantly gratified in February of 1976, when Margaret awoke one fine morning to find her photograph splashed all over the front page of Britain's answer to the *National Enquirer*, the *News of the World*. Unfortunately, the notice that resulted was not the flattering kind.

The pictures in the most flamboyant member of England's "penny press" showed Margaret having a grand time in the Caribbean. Only she wasn't having a grand time alone. She was accompanied by a man nearly two decades her junior, and the photos left no one doubting that Margaret and young Roderick "Roddy" Llewellyn were very chummy indeed.

Little was left to the imagination of anyone glancing at the photographs of Margaret walking on the sands with Roddy, sipping champagne while gazing into his eyes, anointing him (and being stroked in turn) with suntan oil. One person whose imagination was conceivably not soothed by the intimate pictures was a photographer himself. It was an ancestor of Margaret's, Queen Victoria, who made famous the phrase "We are not amused." At this latest go around in their marital follies, Antony Armstrong-Jones, Margaret's husband, was not amused in the slightest. The jig—and the marriage along with it—was up.

It wasn't all that much of a surprise. By 1976, not too many people were ingenuous enough to believe those old stories about princesses living happily ever after, certainly not *this* princess, in any case. Even Margaret herself long ago gave up any pretensions about having anything approaching a normal, conservative, upper-class marriage. Long before her island-nuzzling had hit the front page, the shocking truth about her marriage to Armstrong-Jones had become the cocktail chitchat of the bored aristocracy. It seemed as if *everybody* had something to say about Meg and Tony.

Margaret could have cared less what folks had to say. It was all too much to think about. A friend recalls a discussion of Jacqueline Kennedy's marriage to Aristotle Onassis. "It's the scandal of the century!" gasped the friend in regard to the Onassises' ménage. "No," retorted the princess lightly but firmly. "Tony and I are the scandal of the century."

She wasn't far from wrong.

If their marriage never reached truly scandalous proportions, it's still a fact that Margaret and Tony elicited many a raised eyebrow in their time. But then, raised eyebrows have come Margaret's way ever since that day she tumbled from the perambulator.

She's the Imperfect Princess, Margaret Rose, a shocker from the word go. Just as she fell from that pram, Margaret has been falling in and out of questionable situations ever since. The unpredictable tot has become the imprudent adult, often to the dismay of her peers.

The world of royalty implies perfection, otherworldliness, a realm of magical creatures free from the problems and afflictions with which mere mortals struggle. But Margaret has proved herself unlike this. She is all too human. She has faults and fallibilities to spare.

No one has ever been able to accept Margaret's eccentricities and limitations with the same degree of casualness she herself has always possessed. Even as a child, she had her own number, she knew her game. At her first fancy dress party, the little darling hadn't been able to contain herself when she overheard one of the adult females present remark to a friend, "Oh, what a perfect angel!"

Margaret had felt compelled to set the woman straight immediately. "My mummy," she piped, "says I am a holy terror."

Yes, she was a holy terror, and she still is. Even when enjoying her happiest days, Princess Margaret was always someone to contend with—as when, during the best years of her marriage to Armstrong-Jones, Margaret coldly corrected a friend who'd referred to "Tony" in passing. "Tony?" she murmured, feigning shocked incomprehension. "*Tony?* He's the Earl of Snowdon to you!"

Such haughtiness as Margaret flaunts when dealing with the "commoners" (who can be anyone besides Margaret herself or her sister, the queen) might be more easily accepted if Margaret were a more regal royal lady herself. Considering her own infallibility, both Margaret's friends and enemies consider her holier-than-thou behavior unseemly.

The British have always lived by their own set of rules. In Britain, what one does in one's own private life is considered eminently one's own business. The English will purposefully ignore one's idiosyncrasies, quirks, perversions, and even just plain obnoxiousness. They're all too happy to heap any odd behavior under their famous heading of "eccentricity" while they look the other way. But when a member of the aristocracy, especially one who is living on a sizable income from the queen's privy purse, carries on with a shocking lack of decorum and then doesn't even know enough to keep her mouth shut, well, at that point enough is considered enough.

Handsome young Roddy Llewellyn was in the position of being something of the straw that broke the camel's back. By the time his romance with Margaret had made the papers, more than a few of her compatriots were thrilled to see her get a slap on the wrist. After all, they felt, hadn't she been asking for it for ages? Not even considering lesser dalliances, hadn't her sojourn on the isle of Mustique with Llewellyn been her third such romantic idyll in as many years? Hadn't everyone known for ages that she and Tony were going their separate ways? Who did she think she was, anyway? Wasn't everyone bloody well sick and tired of the princess's desire to be one of the gang one minute and her snooty insistence on being treated as God's chosen the next? There was little sympathy this time for Princess Margaret's making a mess of things.

The Llewellyn situation was more than a mere embarrassment for the country. It precipitated a genuine crisis for the royal family, as the humiliated Antony Armstrong-Jones dashed to Buckingham Palace to insist that the queen either make her sister toe the line and stick to her best behavior or else sanction a legal split. Divorce within the royal family is not unheard of, not *totally*, but it's not par for the course, either. When the queen finally sanctioned a legal separation, it was obvious that Meg and Tony's marriage had been at the very end of its tether. Still, there was little commiseration for Princess Margaret.

Over the years the public felt it had bestowed on her the full measure of its compassion. Now, sympathy was in the direction of the likable husband she had mistreated, the children who would be deeply affected by their parents' break-up, and the queen who was finding her sister to be her own cross. When it came time to dole out the sympathy, Margaret was receiving strictly beggar's rations.

But is scorn and contempt all that Princess Margaret deserves? Is it too late for a little kindness, a bit of understanding? And, if it is, how has she managed to fall so far from the public's favor, this witty woman who was once their darling? To condemn the middle-aged, discontented princess for her outrageous behavior is easy enough; to comprehend the motivations that have driven her is difficult—but more just.

All men and women deserve to be judged by the same set of standards, but Margaret's position in this world has affected her entire life to such a degree that it's impossible to weigh her actions without taking into consideration her standing in life. It's impossible to look at the woman without looking at her title, albeit as a princess she has fallen far, far below story-book standards. No, she isn't untouchable or larger than life or even a particular credit to her country. What she is, instead, is the disgruntled, frustrated, aging woman who was once a spoiled, lonely, and undeniably charming little girl. And it's important to remember that she was a princess then as she is a princess now. More than for the rest of the world, her birthright has determined the rules of her existence. One can overcome being born poor or even being born unloved. One can never overcome being born into royalty.

Destiny is a strange and complex force, and only the most extreme fatalists would insist that one has no control whatsoever over the circumstances of life. On the other hand, no one's actions are independent of his or her past. In Margaret's case, a lifetime of smaller indiscretions led inevitably to the scandal that would erupt in photos showing her rubbing suntan oil into the back of a twenty-eight-year-old man. It led to the startling headlines announcing her romance with the handsome, socially connected hippie who wore a gold ring through his ear. It led to the shattering of her marriage vows and to the disrespect of the public. It led to the sad and all-too-common middle age of what had once been a very special and always royal life.

Chapter One

Princess Margaret, like her sister Queen Elizabeth II, inherited her beautiful eyes, her clear skin, and her dazzling smile from her mother. The Queen Mother, a striking-looking woman even in her mid-seventies, was a beautiful child who grew into a breathtaking young woman and the perfect choice for a king's consort. Though she was a commoner by rights, and though a special act of Parliament was needed before her husband was allowed to marry her, there is not and never has been anything in the least common about the woman who was born Elizabeth Bowes-Lyon.

She was born on August 4, 1900, the youngest but one of ten children of the fourteenth earl of Strathmore. Elizabeth was born at St. Paul's Walden Bury in Hertfordshire, but she was to spend only her first four years in that bright, sunny area. In 1904, when her father inherited both his title as earl of Strathmore and Glamis Castle, the family moved to Scotland—and to one of history's most mysterious mansions.

Glamis (pronounced Glarms) Castle was the seat of the earls of Strathmore and had a history no other castle could rival. It dated back to the thirteenth century; there are frequent references to Glamis in the records of that time. Perhaps its greatest glory was being referred to by Shakespeare, in *Macbeth*. Glamis, in that play, is held to have been the scene of Duncan's murder.

Built of sandstone, with original walls that measured eight feet thick, Glamis was said to be the oldest inhabited residence in Great Britain. It was also rumored to be inhabited by a ghost or two.

Little Elizabeth's closest friend during childhood was her younger brother David. Both were far too full of fun and merriment to worry about ghosts, and they thought all the haunting business was a bit of a giggle. For the most part, that is. There were times when the Bowes-Lyon children were much more afraid of the possibility of specters than they'd admit to each other.

There was reason to respect the ghostly rumors. One room at Glamis was called the Hangman's Room because two ghost-visited guests had hanged themselves there. Even as reputable an authority as Sir Walter Scott had succumbed to the terror that was Glamis. In 1814 he had spent a night there and written, "I was conducted to my apartments in a distant part of the building. I must admit that when I heard door after door shut after my conductor had retired, I began to consider myself as too far from the living, and somewhat too near the dead."

If all this hadn't steeped Glamis in enough historical importance, there was also the fact that Bonnie Prince Charlie, the Young Pretender, had sought shelter at Glamis in 1746, when hiding from his pursuers. A sword and some of the young prince's clothing were enshrined in the castle ever afterwards and certainly served to give Elizabeth Bowes-Lyon, the future queen of England, a sense of the historical importance of her own ancestors.

Not that there was ever any reason for the young Elizabeth to even imagine she would one day take residence at Buckingham Palace. It was beyond her wildest dreams. And, indeed, she would arrive there only through the most perverse machinations of fate.

When Elizabeth was five years old she met a nine-year-old boy named Bertie. He would one day be her husband and the king of England, but, at the time, both were more than one step removed from the throne. The year was 1905. That freewheeling playboy, Edward VII, who brought us the merry Edwardians, was still king. Bertie's father, George V, wouldn't take the throne for another five years. The occasion of this meeting between Elizabeth and Albert was a children's birthday party given by the countess of Leicester in London.

At age nine, little Albert's bloodlines were indeed impressive. His father was heir to the throne, and he himself would be second in line to succeed his father one day (after his older brother David). Personalitywise, however, little Bertie wasn't apt to impress anybody. He was a pale, painfully shy little boy, frail by nature, already suffering from the gastritis which would plague him in adulthood. And he was afflicted with a frightful stammer that would be overcome only by years of intense work with a noted speech therapist.

Elizabeth was just the opposite. An outgoing, beautiful child with bright eyes and cascading hair, she was, even at five, the belle of the ball. The personality that would later endear her to millions of subjects was already in the formative stage. With a wisdom unheard of in children her age, she went out of her way to be kind and attentive to the awkward, shy little boy. It was almost as if she understood all the humiliations he endured. These included having his own father fly into rages over his speech impediment, being forced to write with his right hand when he was actually left-handed, and living in the shadow of his big brother David who was already becoming noted for his magnetism and charisma.

It would be years before Bertie and Elizabeth

met again. By that time, World War I had been fought and ended, Bertie's father was king, and Bertie himself was the duke of York. But Bertie was still much the same—a shy, stuttering young man uncomfortable in most social situations.

Albert lacked certain worldly qualities, but he had his share of others. He was handsome, very much resembling his elder brother David, with the same Germanic good looks. The royal family were descended from the House of Hanover, through George I, a German who ruled in the early eighteenth century (and spoke no English!). The family's original surname of Guelph had been changed to Windsor in 1917, during the height of anti-German sentiment in Great Britain. The name may have gone, but the German bone structure and physiognomy remained.

Elizabeth had a true sense of style. She was always a fashionable dresser (though as Queen Mother, she has been mostly notable for her dowdiness), and her fringed hairdo set the standard in her crowd for years. She was also a great socializer, never at a loss for words, at ease in any situation. She adored parties and had a great fondness for dancing, two tastes she would pass on to her younger daughter.

But Elizabeth was no flighty social butterfly. She had a good head on her shoulders and a surplus of old-fashioned common sense. She was soft-spoken, with faultless bearing and impeccable manners, distinctions which, along with her diminutive size, would later earn her the public nickname of "The Dainty Duchess."

One thing Elizabeth and Bertie had in common was their love of sports and games. The young duke loved horses, as did Elizabeth. She was also a fishing fan and never averse to roughing it on hunting or hiking expeditions.

And so Bertie and Elizabeth began seeing each other. He was courting her in earnest and was soon madly in love with her. But Elizabeth, while fond of her swain, would not agree to marriage.

Elizabeth had no interest in getting involved with the royal family. As a matter of fact, she had a positive aversion to it. Though there was barely an inkling at that time of a kingship in the wings for Bertie, he was still duke of York. And as a duke, he would be expected to bear a heavy social burden, making appearances at various functions and fulfilling his obligations in representing the crown. Elizabeth had no desire to be by his side in the limelight. She considered herself much too private a person to get involved with a schedule of personal appearances and responsibilities.

Elizabeth, it seemed, was bent on being an immovable object, but she had not yet reckoned with the irresistible force of the power behind the throne. King George V's wife, Queen Mary, was Elizabeth's greatest admirer, and she made no secret of her desire that the young woman marry her son. On the contrary, she practically launched a campaign to get Elizabeth and Bertie hitched!

The dowager queen spent much time with Elizabeth, pointing out Bertie's finer qualities, calling attention to his conscientiousness, his kindness, his dependability. But the queen's urgings appeared to be of no avail. When Bertie finally got the nerve to propose, Elizabeth turned him down, just as she had already turned down several other marriage proposals from an assortment of eligible beaux.

Elizabeth didn't want to hurt Bertie's feelings. She was still just as conscious of his vulnerability as she'd been when they were both children at the birthday party. She explained that it wasn't marriage to Bertie she wished to avoid, but the burden of becoming royalty. She told him in all honesty how she dreaded even the thought of having to attend all those official functions. Bertie accepted her refusal with no bitterness, but was more determined than ever to keep up his patient pursuit until he won the lady's hand.

And he did win the lovely Elizabeth. In 1923 Bertie again asked her to be his bride. As he went off to Elizabeth's home to propose, Bertie was reminded by George V that if Elizabeth accepted, he'd be a lucky man indeed. Bertie was well aware of this, and he wasted no time in sending word to his father as soon as his proposal had been accepted. The ecstatic Albert went straight to the telegraph office to relay the happy news to the king. In typical succinctness he sent a wire stating simply: "ALL RIGHT. BERTIE."

The special act of Parliament which would

allow Bertie to marry a commoner was considered a mere formality and it went through with no problems whatsoever. On April 26, 1923, the two were joined in holy matrimony.

The address made at the ceremony by Dr. Lang, the archbishop of York, predicted with uncanny prescience the deep relationship the couple would have. "Your lives are now, till death, made one," he told them. "You cannot resolve that your wedded life shall be happy. But you can and will resolve that it shall be noble. You will think not so much of joy as of achievement. You will have a great ambition to make this one life now given to you something rich and true and beautiful."

The words were stunningly prophetic of a marriage spent in partnership and service to the throne—a throne to which neither Bertie nor Elizabeth ever aspired. Though their life together began with a speech about duty, they weren't to know until much later just how much duty would eventually demand of them.

As the duke and duchess of York enjoyed the first calm, peaceful years of their marriage, they had no reason to believe they would ever live closer to Buckingham Palace than 145 Piccadilly. That was the address of the home which they discovered after their first year of marriage, the home where princesses Elizabeth and Margaret would spend the first years of their lives.

When the duke and duchess first inspected the premises on Piccadilly, they had to use their imaginations in earnest. They were greeted by a dilapidated hulk of a building with twenty-five bedrooms angling off long, dusty corridors. After deciding to sign a crown lease for the property (which they began to occupy in 1927), Bertie and Elizabeth began extensive renovation to make the house a comfortable home.

Walls had to be knocked down. Rooms were fused together to form larger quarters. The final result was a showplace, which was unfortunately destroyed during the Second World War. But while it stood, 145 Piccadilly was a fine home, with a spacious nursery and solarium occupying practically an entire floor, and with lush, manicured grounds.

The proximity to Buckingham Palace was a major plus as far as the couple were concerned. Their house overlooked the palace gardens and allowed Bertie to be close at hand to his parents. Of course, neither Bertie nor Elizabeth had the slightest idea that the arrival on British shores of a lady from Baltimore would catapult them from Piccadilly to the palace.

The wheels that were to convey them were set in motion in November, 1930, at an otherwise innocuous English country house party. The Prince of Wales, heir to the throne, was introduced to an attractive American who had recently taken up residence in London. Wallis Warfield Simpson was thirty-four at the time and wed to her second husband. The prince was thirty-six and a bachelor. He was immediately captivated by the lady he would later term "the most independent woman" he had ever met.

The fact that he immediately found Mrs. Simpson fascinating didn't propel David into a sudden relationship with her. He didn't start seriously seeing Wallis Simpson until 1934, after she had broken with her second husband. By that time Wallis had also revised her opinion of the prince. If she hadn't been inclined to remain open-minded regarding her first impression of David Windsor, it's doubtful that the most scandalous romance of the 1930s would ever have gotten off the ground.

When David and Wallis first chatted at that country party, it was not a scintillating conversation. The prince, in attempting to make pleasant small talk, had asked Mrs. Simpson whether she missed central heating now that she was residing in London. The lady was never one for small talk. "Every American woman who comes to your country is always asked that same question," she replied. "I had hoped for something more original from the Prince of Wales."

She was, of course, to obtain something much more original—the unqualified love of the man who would become King Edward VIII. In the early part of the thirties, as the prince began steadily courting Mrs. Simpson, members of the royal family were despairing over the entire affair, which Queen Mary, the prince's mother, once summed up to Prime Minister Stanley Baldwin as "a pretty kettle of fish."

Within his family, knowledge was certain that King George V's health was poor. In fact, it was considered that his health was failing so rapidly he might not even live to see his Jubilee in 1935. He did survive, however, and on May 6, 1935, King George V and Queen Mary rode in a glass carriage amongst their subjects, in celebration of twenty-five years of their rule.

In the meantime, the prince, heir to the throne, had begun seeing Mrs. Simpson with frightening regularity. By 1935 the two were openly traveling together, staying at a Tyrolean hotel, journeying to Vienna, Budapest, Corsica. As the prince's ailing father watched the romance blossom, his heart filled with sorrow.

"After I am dead," George V predicted sadly, "the boy will ruin himself in twelve months." And it would be, in fact, eleven months after King George V's death on January 20, 1936 that King Edward VIII would abdicate his throne to his brother Bertie.

The months between King George V's funeral and that fateful day—January 20, 1936—were tumultuous ones indeed. These were days that would leave their imprint on the pages of British history forever and affect the life and destiny of the little Princess Margaret Rose.

During the period between his father's death and his scheduled coronation, David, who took the name King Edward VIII, wasn't winning many friends in government circles. He was popular with the people, yes, but the people's choice isn't always what matters. In Parliament's point of view, Edward VIII had been taking too many public stands for a member of royalty, since it's always been considered best for monarchs to be seen but not heard, so to speak. The rulers of the British Isles, since the time of Cromwell, have been a far cry from the absolute monarchs of old. As king, David was expected to keep his opinions muffled, to be nonpartisan, nonpolitical, attractive but harmless.

Instead, David tended to say just what he thought time and again, much to the dismay of his Parliament. When he visited Wales and sympathized volubly with the impoverished striking miners, public sympathy and sentiment for him swelled. The attitude behind the closed doors of his ministers, however, was that King Edward VIII was on the verge of pushing his luck. He wasn't, many felt, the best choice for king.

Still, kings were born, not chosen, so there really wasn't any choice in the matter. Edward VIII's continuing affair with the two-time divorcée from the States was just salt in the wounds of his ministers. After a photograph was printed showing the new king and Mrs. Simpson sailing on his yacht, with her hand possessively grasping his wrist, any doubts one might have had as to the seriousness of their relationship vanished.

After that, it didn't take long before word spread that King Edward VIII was Mrs. Simpson's absolute slave. Well and good—*that* was considered his personal business. But the public case was that he would soon have to make a choice and decide what to do about his future. He couldn't go on as king, openly flaunting his relationship with the American woman, without in some way justifying his actions.

It was generally considered that the king had three possible roads to follow. He could defy his ministers by proposing to Wallis Simpson, marrying her and saying his ministers be damned. In this case, he would be doing more than pushing his luck with Parliament, he'd be shoving it. And Great Britain would undoubtedly be plunged into a major governmental crisis.

The second course the king could choose would be to marry Mrs. Simpson morganatically; that is, make her his legal wife but not attempt to make her his queen. In that case, any children the two might have would not be in line for succession to the throne.

The third choice open to the king was, of course, the one his ministers most fervently hoped he would make—to simply renounce Mrs. Simpson and begin behaving in the manner deemed proper for monarchs.

One person who remained quite unsympathetic towards the king and his lady-friend in this affair was the quietly disapproving duchess of York. When she had married into royalty, the duchess had wholeheartedly embraced the tenets thereof; the petite yet powerful duchess took the duties and obligations of the throne seriously. She felt Edward VIII owed much more to his people than his behavior was supplying. She certainly didn't think Wally Simpson was deserving of a place in the family into which she, the duchess, had married.

And yet it wasn't all so black and white for Elizabeth. She had nothing against Wallis Simpson personally. When she met her, she found the other woman quite pleasant. And she was concerned that, in the end, her brother-in-law might do exactly what he eventually did. That is, renounce not Mrs. Simpson but his monarchy, leaving Bertie holding the bag—and wearing the crown.

These were fateful days for the Yorks, since the last vestiges of the privacy they so valued were now hanging in the balance. Bertie had no desire to rule Britannia. Elizabeth was even more strongly opposed to the idea. And Bertie realized that, in many ways, he was ill equipped for the job.

George V had never been a doting father to his sons. He had never bothered to explain the details of kingship to his second eldest. Bertie, as duke of York, had been left out of every area of crucial decision making. He had little idea how things were done, business carried on, the empire ruled.

Not that Bertie's late father had lavished all his interest and attention on the more vivacious, fun-loving Prince of Wales. No, even David was sadly lacking in understanding the duties of the throne. Certainly this was one reason for his difficulties as Edward VIII.

Nevertheless, equipped or not, as the final months of 1936 drew closer, it became more clear that Bertie would be king.

In a historic radio broadcast on December 11, 1936, the world listened as King Edward VIII abdicated to his younger brother Albert, who took the name King George VI. It was a fateful day, and one person who was not made happier for it was the duchess of York. She became Queen Elizabeth upon Edward's abdication. But as the archbishop of York had stated at her marriage, her thoughts could not be only of her own personal joy. A life of achievement—a noble life—was more important by far.

King Edward VIII's halting voice reached millions from Windsor Castle, as he broadcast his decision to give up the throne for the woman he loved. With great emotion, he concluded: "...now that I have been succeeded by my brother, the duke of York, my first words must be to declare my allegiance to him. This I do with all my heart.... He has one matchless blessing, enjoyed by so many of you and not bestowed on me—a happy home with his wife and children. ... Now we all have a new king. I wish him, and you, his people, happiness and prosperity with all my heart. God bless you all. God save the king!"

With those words, David relinquished his title of King Edward VIII, and his right to rule. He went immediately into exile, sailing off in the night to rendezvous with Mrs. Simpson on the Continent, where he would marry her the following summer. He did not return to his own country until after the outbreak of World War II.

Immediately upon being declared king and taking the name of his father, Bertie gave his predecessor a brand-new title. His first act as King George VI was to designate his brother David the duke of Windsor.

And so, Great Britain had a new king and queen. In his first speech as king, Bertie told his subjects, "The queen and I will always keep in our hearts the importance of this day. May we ever be worthy of the good will which, I am proud to think, surrounds us at the outset of my reign...."

There *was* good will. Britain had a new king and queen, and the entire country received them with an eager joy. Britishers were ready to have a "normal" couple helming their country. As Elizabeth and Bertie stood gazing out at the cheering throng immediately following the coronation, the new queen consort turned to her husband and gently remarked, "They seem to like us."

Their subjects did indeed like Bertie and Elizabeth. But they weren't the whole show at the coronation. Sharing the attention and adoration of the crowd were two little girls who had already won the public's hearts and admiration. The era of Margaret and Elizabeth—the adorable Little Princesses—was about to begin.

Chapter Two

The duke and duchess of York had already welcomed both their children into the world by the time Edward VIII's abdication jolted the populace and made way for his younger brother to become king. Fittingly enough, Princess Margaret's arrival in the world was one of the most notable of all royal births. Circumstances led Margaret to create quite a stir before she'd even howled her first cry of life.

The public had already taken the duchess of York's first child to their hearts. Elizabeth had been delivered of her little namesake (now Queen Elizabeth II) by Caesarean section on the 21st of April, 1926. The baby was a hit with the press from the start, heralding the beginning of five decades of publicity for the fascinating sisters.

So popular was the new baby that Bertie even joked ruefully, "My chief claim to fame seems to be that I am the father of Princess Elizabeth." It wouldn't be long before the duke of York discovered that, if having one darling girl was a guarantee of acceptance by the public, having two was tantamount to holding the key to the world's heart.

The first inkling most Britons had that a second baby was on the way came in April, 1930, when the Buckingham Palace court circular announced, "The duchess of York has cancelled her forthcoming engagements and she is not undertaking any further functions during the summer."

It wasn't difficult for the Dainty Duchess's fans to read between the lines of that announcement and realize there was a baby brother or sister on the way for little Elizabeth, who was already known by her nickname, Lilibet.

It was expected that the duchess would choose to give birth to her second child at home, which was then 145 Piccadilly. She had remained in London for the birth of her first daughter, spending her confinement at her parents' home in Bruton Street. So it was quite a surprise to everyone when Elizabeth announced her decision to arrange matters so that her second child would be born, not in England, but in Scotland, at her own girlhood home, Glamis Castle.

The new baby would thereby be the first royal infant since Charles I (who was born in 1600) to be born on Scottish soil. The announcement occasioned great joy with the proud Scots. But not *everyone* was pleased with the news.

One person who had no cause to be ecstatic at the news that the impending birth would take place at Glamis was Mr. J. R. Clynes, the Home Secretary. Archaic custom had it that the Home Secretary should be in attendance at all royal births—a practice originally intended to protect against cradle-switching of royal infants. Clynes was faced with the gloomy prospect of spending days sequestered on the moors, just to guarantee his presence immediately after the baby's arrival.

After all the trouble this outmoded convention was to cause at the time of Margaret's birth, it's easy to understand why Bertie, as King George VI, later declared the presence of the Home Secretary at a royal birth as unnecessary. He put an end to it. Mr. Clynes was the last British official to face the dilemma which awaited him upon his arrival at Glamis.

The problem was that the daughter who would prove so impetuous in later life was in no hurry to be born. Clynes arrived in Scotland on the 4th day of August, the thirtieth birthday of the duchess of York, who was already ensconced in Glamis Castle to await the arrival of her baby. The duke of York, who had felt right from the start that the presence of the Home Secretary was an absurdity, had an aversion to sharing his lodgings with the man. So Mr. Clynes was billeted down the road at Airlie Castle, where Queen Mary's close friend Lady Airlie proved to be the most gracious of hostesses under conditions that must have dearly tried her hospitality.

Both Mr. Clynes and Lady Airlie had expected that he would be an occupant of Airlie Castle for a matter of mere days. But, even in the womb, Margaret was exercising the prerogatives of a princess. One day melted away to the next as the pages were anxiously turned on Mr. Clynes's calendar. And the duchess of York had nary a labor pain.

As the 15th, then the 16th, then the 17th of August passed by, Mr. Clynes's imperturbable British decorum was properly shaken. He had now been a houseguest at Airlie Castle for two entire weeks, and he felt that his prolonged presence was by now an embarrassment and an affront to the duchess. So, the better to protect the feelings of both the Yorks, he began spending most of his energy avoiding the duchess, as well as trying to stay out of Lady Airlie's way. It was a bit of a farce.

As one might imagine, Clynes's joy was nearly as great as the Yorks' when, at 9:22 P.M. on August 21, 1930, the duchess was delivered, by Caesarean section, of a six-pound eleven-ounce baby girl. To Clynes, the happy news brought visions not of layettes and perambulators, but of swift passage back to London for himself!

The birth of a royal infant has always been cause for rejoicing, and little Margaret's birth was no exception. As news of the baby's arrival spread, crowds began pouring into the area of

Glamis from all over Scotland, coming from as far afield as Aberdeen and Edinburgh. On the Glamis hillside, a huge beacon was lit to honor the birth. Back in England, the baby was heralded by a forty-one-gun salute from the Tower of London, followed by yet another salute from the guns of the Royal Horse Artillery in Hyde Park.

The air of exalted celebration was further enhanced when the bells of Westminster Abbey pealed in greeting. People on the streets hailed each other with the cheerful news. It was a happy day for most Britons, who had already been won over by the family of the man who would one day rule them.

The first public bulletin pertaining to the baby was issued by the duchess's attending surgeon, Sir Henry Simson, just a few days after the birth. It stated:

"Her hair is of a tint between light and medium brown. The shape of her lips already shows a marked resemblance to that of her mother's. She is a remarkably contented baby, but when she does cry, she gives proof of her possession of lusty lungs."

No one was more pleased with the new arrival than was her own sister. Princess Elizabeth was four years and four months old when the new baby was born. Characteristically, she showed little jealousy over the new arrival. Her first action as a big sister was to carry some of her favorite toys into the room where the baby lay and to heap them around her new sister's cot. Little Elizabeth seemed to be quite pleased with her good fortune in having acquired a sibling.

Margaret's behavior at this point was just as characteristic (in retrospect) as Elizabeth's. She caused her first bit of tumult just three days after her birth. On that day, a Mrs. Gevina Brown gave birth to a child. Mrs. Brown was puzzled when she received a notice from the Glamis registrar in the shortest time imaginable, asking her to please register her son's birth as soon as possible. Mrs. Brown knew it wasn't her newborn George who was responsible for all this haste. There was a different force behind this pressure to register the baby.

The force was the little infant born to the duke and duchess of York. The impetus was superstition.

When Bertie had gone into the village proper at Glamis to register his new daughter's birth, he got a rather rude surprise. The next child to be put in the registrar's official book would be opposite that unluckiest of numbers—13!

Now, Bertie was somewhat of a superstitious sort, as was the duchess, so he made a deal with the registrar. He would wait to register his baby daughter until after another baby was born in the neighborhood. That way, the next baby could take the unwanted slot at number 13, and the Yorks' daughter could go down in the books at number 14.

Years later, however, Gevina Brown, who went along with it all at the time, admitted she wasn't too thrilled about being stuck with this dubious distinction. "I was a little unhappy at registering George under number thirteen," she said, "although I am not a superstitious person. However, I knew that if I delayed my registration, the duchess would do the same thing, so I decided to sign the book there and then and clear the way for the princess's parents. But I have no regrets. The duchess, as she was then, is a charming person and spoke to us often as we cut through the castle grounds on the way to church on Sundays."

And so, the baby of the duke and duchess of York, in reality the thirteenth baby born into the Glamis registry for that period, was legally registered as the fourteenth. It was an effort at keeping ill luck from plaguing her footsteps. (In retrospect it might be deemed less than successful.)

Practically speaking, the formality of the tot's birth registration was only the first of several considerations. Naming the child was also a priority. And it was not necessarily the easiest thing to accomplish.

The duchess first thought of naming the child Ann Margaret, feeling that name would go well with her sister's. But the name of Ann never panned out, mainly due to the dissatisfaction of King George V.

The duchess's in-laws were very much to be considered when it came to choosing names. The power of George V and Mary can never be underestimated. As long as these monarchs lived, they each exercised considerable influence over the affairs of their children. Queen Mary was an iron-willed woman who continued to rule her family even after her husband's death. When Lilibet and Margaret were of schooling age, their governess would receive detailed letters of instruction from the dowager queen, with specific suggestions as to the course of the girls' education. As for King George V, he was quite the martinet, a man who knew what he wanted, *when* he wanted it, and who had never been given to flexibility. George V did *not* care for the name Ann.

So Bertie and Elizabeth dropped the idea of naming the baby Ann Margaret and began trying different combinations of names on each other, struggling to come up with something that would please the two of them as well as Bertie's parents.

The duke and duchess finally decided on Margaret Rose. This name, happily, met with the king's approval as well. It paid tribute to one of the duchess' favorite people, her sister, Lady Rose Bowes-Lyon. As an older child, Margaret was to drop her middle name, but in early childhood she was always referred to, in public at least, by both her names.

At ten weeks of age, Princess Margaret Rose was christened by the archbishop of Canterbury, Dr. Lang. In the family tradition, she wore the robe of Spitalfields silk and Hamilton lace that had been used for all royal baptisms since the first-born of her great-grandmother Queen Victoria had been christened. The lilyfont was also a tradition; gold-plated and imposing, it had been brought up from Windsor for the occasion. The flagon of Jordan water used in the ceremony was also a tradition. It came from Palestine—at that time a troubled, British-administered territory.

And so Princess Margaret Rose arrived in Great Britain, a beautiful, magical child right from the start, born to a handsome, popular couple, sister to an extremely well liked little girl, resident of a spacious, sun-drenched nursery populated by more than thirty toy hobby-horses.

Little Margaret Rose would never lack for attention. There was a staff of three at 145 Piccadilly to take care of the nursery chores for herself and Lilibet. There was Clara Knight, the head nanny, a kindly woman who had been the duchess of York's own nanny. She was nicknamed "Alah" because as a child Elizabeth couldn't pronounce the name Clara. Then there was Margaret MacDonald, the assistant nanny, a capable young Scotswoman in her mid-twenties, who would remain in the royal household to become the dresser for Lilibet when she was crowned Queen Elizabeth II. And there was also Margaret MacDonald's little sister, nursemaid Ruby MacDonald. She came to the York household as a young girl of sixteen and remained with Princess Margaret through adulthood, staying on even after the princess had wed Antony Armstrong-Jones and taken up residence at

Kensington Palace. Ruby left Margaret's employ only after the birth of the princess's son, Viscount Linley.

Later, these three women were joined by a fourth. Margaret Crawford was hired as governess to the girls when both were very small. She was the Little Princesses' governess and dearest friend for many years, leaving only to marry shortly before Lilibet's own wedding. "Crawfie," as she was called, was well liked by the royal family and even presented with a grace-and-favor cottage by King George VI upon her marriage. Still, her decision to publish her memoirs of the years with the princesses, after she left the employ of the king and queen, didn't sit well with the family. The volume remains the definitive tale of the Little Princesses' upbringing, since it was Miss Crawford who had the most intimate contact with the two girls during their youth.

It was a period amply recorded by all the journals of the time. What better copy could there be than the pintsized Margaret and her lissome older sister? Both Lilibet and Margaret Rose were considered highly quotable, though everyone soon agreed it was Margaret who showed the most wit. Lilibet's stock in trade was kindness and consideration, not coyness and a quick retort. She remains the same to this day.

It's typical of Elizabeth that she greeted the news of having a baby sister with the announcement, "I shall let her ride Peggy," referring to her own Shetland pony. It was considered the supreme gesture that she should offer the new arrival the use of her most treasured possession.

Indeed, Elizabeth was an unassuming, generous little girl. And all of her noble qualities would be much needed in the years to come. Not only was she going to grow up to be queen of England—she was also going to have to adjust to the nerve-shattering, demanding role of being madcap Margaret's big sister.

Chapter Three

What was life like for little Margaret Rose and her sister Elizabeth? For both of them, childhood was a magical time. For both of them, youth was divided into two periods—the days before their papa became king and the years after he ascended to the throne.

For Margaret, it would appear that Uncle David's abdication and Papa's taking the throne were less important than they were to Lilibet who was catapulted to the position of heiress presumptive. Still, Margaret was far from untouched by the chain of events her father's new office would set in motion. In fact, it affected her greatly and had much bearing on the heartache she would endure later in life.

Albert was plain "Papa" to his children,

although to his youngest daughter he was a god. Margaret was her daddy's girl right from the start. She adored Papa, and it was around the shy, withdrawn Bertie as opposed to the more outgoing, sociable Elizabeth that their younger daughter's life revolved. She was the satellite to his sun.

But Bertie had never been cut out to play the sun, and little Margaret's hero worship at times embarrassed him. Never a man given to public displays of affection, reserved and stand-offish, Bertie would sometimes be at a loss when Margaret Rose literally tackled him as he walked through the front door of 145 Piccadilly. She would hurl herself at him, encircling his legs with her plump little arms, clinging to him like the proverbial piece of flypaper.

Margaret's enthusiasm worked. Everyone knew that the shy Bertie had a special soft spot in his heart for his younger child. Her displays of warmth and adoration ruffled him, but they never annoyed him. On the contrary, his flustered exterior on these occasions only served to hide the happiness her love brought to him.

Margaret was both loved and lovable as a child. Her stolid father wasn't the only one who was quick to melt in the presence of her fiery charisma. Margaret Rose was a natural-born charmer, and there were few who escaped falling under her spell.

Papa wasn't the only major force in Margaret's life. The influence of Lilibet on her sister can never be overestimated. She was probably the most important person in Margaret's childhood, and the trust and dependency Margaret feels towards Queen Elizabeth II today is a continuation of their all-important childhood roles.

With little more than four years difference in their ages, Lilibet and Margaret shared a twinlike affinity when growing up. They were together constantly during their earliest years. The story of one sister's childhood is necessarily the story of the other's first years as well.

As an only child, Lilibet's favorite game had always been one she'd played with her parents. It was called "The Three Bears." When playing with the duke and duchess, Lilibet would be the Little Bear, her mother would be the Rather Big Bear, and Papa was the Big Bear. After Margaret's birth, Lilibet happily announced "Now we can play *Four* Bears. The baby will be the Very Little Bear."

Margaret was a very gifted baby. Her intelligence and native talents made themselves known while she was still in swaddling clothes.

For instance, it was apparent very early in the game that Margaret had inherited her mother's love of music and her grandmother Queen Mary's musical ear. Margaret was still just a baby when the duchess of York's mother, Lady Strathmore, made the most amazing discovery. Margaret's maternal grandmother was carrying the baby down the stairs at Glamis and listening to the tot's la-la-las when she suddenly realized that Margaret Rose wasn't making the usual infant's cooing, senseless sounds. Instead, she was humming a perfect rendition of the "Merry Widow" waltz. The entire family was suitably impressed with Baby Margaret's natural talents. Little did they realize her precocity was just beginning.

Yes, the older she got, the more Margaret tended to enjoy shocking those around her. She was generally a delightful child, beautiful and bouncy, cute as a button with her tousled chestnut curls framing the most perfect of British peaches-and-cream complexions and with her bright blue eyes impishly surveying the world. She was quite a handful, and adults would sometimes lose patience with Margaret. But she would always manage to win them back over to her camp.

The Little Princesses were favorites with all their relatives. After the family celebration of his 42nd wedding anniversary, King George V even admitted, "All the children looked so nice, but none prettier than Lilibet and Margaret." Still, Margaret's dour grandfather usually found her a bit too rambunctious for his personal taste. He preferred spending his time with the older, more thoughtful Lilibet, who was truly his favorite grandchild.

The years preceding 1936 were carefree, happy ones for the two girls. They were far enough removed from the throne that it didn't infringe too greatly upon their lives. Of course, even when Bertie was just the duke of York, his rank kept the girls from having anything resembling a normal upbringing. Times have changed, and today royalty is brought up in a much more relaxed manner. But in those days, children of royalty were handled with kid gloves. And so Lilibet and Margaret, even in their days at 145 Piccadilly, were tutored privately and never mingled with the children of the hoi polloi.

The children's favorite place to play was at Windsor, where they had free run of what was called "The Little House," a scaled-down thatched cottage just the perfect size for two little girls. Here they played house and practiced homemaking, perfecting skills they would never really need. Interestingly, Margaret was quite the hausfrau. She loved scouring the sinks, scrubbing the floors and making little "toy"-sized meals for herself and Lilibet.

When Margaret was just one year old, the Yorks had begun renovating the Royal Lodge at Windsor, and much of her childhood was spent there. The Lodge was a small but lovely cluster of buildings in the middle of Great Windsor Park. It was the former home of George V's racing manager, and just the right size for a summer retreat. The sprawling, wooded grounds were ideal for a family that so loved seclusion. Bertie and Elizabeth liked nothing better than to escape to the Lodge with their children, to picnic, go shooting, hike in the woods, and ride their horses.

Margaret was always very much her own person. Since she was to the manor born, it was of prime importance that Margaret learn, at the earliest possible age, the fundamentals of manners and gentility. Getting her to behave was sometimes frustrating, but since Margaret was going to be leading her life in public, she would have to be taught to mind her p's & q's.

Those who led more normal lives during childhood might find it difficult to envision making one's first appearance at a public ceremonial at the early age of four. But that's how old Margaret was when she attended the wedding, in Westminster Abbey, of her Uncle George, the duke of Kent, and the sophisticated Princess Marina, who would later become Margaret's very favorite aunt. Imagine the self-control and good breeding necessary for a toddler to remain composed during such long and often excruciatingly boring affairs.

Of course, Margaret being Margaret, she strayed from the straight and narrow path more than once, and she could find it difficult, if not impossible, to always mind her royal manners. Margaret would be a devil one minute, an angel the next. As soon as she had irritated adults with her uncontrollable deviltry, she would turn around and soothe them with her ready smile and laughing eyes.

Margaret could practically dare adults to stay peeved with her. She would use all her wiles to appease those angry with her, pulling out all the stops until she got them to smile. The result was that all but her most unforgivable pranks would be quickly laughed away. It was well nigh impossible to stay mad at Margaret, and even the indomitable governess Miss Crawford often worried that she was a pushover for her tiny charge. At her most furious, Miss Crawford could be dissolved into forgiving smiles when little Margaret jumped up and down in front of her demanding "Crawfie! Laugh!"

The wise Lilibet realized early on that Margaret tended to get away with much more than was good for her. But Lilibet certainly couldn't discipline her little sister all by herself. "I really don't know what we are going to do with Margaret, Crawfie," she would worriedly remark to their governess time and again. Even though just a child herself, Lilibet already suspected her sister's impetuousness might one day be her downfall.

Nor were pranks and high jinks Margaret's only diversion. She wanted attention, and there was always more than one way to get it. Mischief on the one hand, talent on the other. Margaret loved entertaining, and she was a natural at it. She made the world her audience. She was an excellent dancer even as a child, and her natural musical gifts developed even more as she grew older. With her gift of perfect pitch, Margaret was often called upon to sing. She never shunned the limelight. Besides having a great voice and a natural affinity for the piano, Margaret was also a born mimic who loved to wow her audience with impressions of Bing Crosby and Burl Ives. Under any circumstances, she emerged a ham.

It has been speculated that, if she hadn't been a princess, Margaret might have ended up going on the stage or devoting her life to show business in some other manner. It isn't easy, or fair, to attempt to weigh the validity of "if onlys." But the truth is that show business and entertainment have always been Margaret's first loves, even as a child she adored the ballet, movies, records, television, while showing little interest in the more typical avocations of her family—raising Corgi dogs and riding horses.

Some people used to say that Margaret seemed more like her Uncle David's child than the offspring of Bertie and Elizabeth. She certainly had the Prince of Wales's love of showfolk and a good time. All through his life, David Windsor was chummy with the entertainment world. He was on best-friend terms with such stars of the thirties as Noel Coward and Bea Lillie, and he was always eager for an opening night, a dinner, a party.

Margaret's father was surely not a social lion. He was much more involved with shooting, fishing and riding. And her mother was devoted to her Corgis and her horses, interests Lilibet would also develop as she grew older. Lilibet's very first crush, as a matter of fact, was on Owen, Buckingham Palace's groom. Owen, who delighted in taking the Little Princess riding, was a far cry from the man she would grow up to marry. Prince Philip does *not* share his wife's passion for horses and the racetrack. "I'm bored stiff by it," admits the husband of today's turf-oriented monarch.

Margaret lost none of her interests as she grew older. She still loves the ballet, the theater, having celebrity friends and going to wham-bang parties. And Lilibet? The rather matronly child grew up to be the rather dowdy matron who loves her children, her dogs and her horses and whose hobbies include playing Scrabble, doing crossword puzzles and watching the telly in bed. The two sisters' paths were never headed in the same direction, regardless of how close they were in each other's affections.

The impish Margaret had her serious side. She had a deep religious bent in childhood, one which would stay with her into young adulthood. In fact, the first book Margaret managed to read by herself, at age five or so, was *Tales of the Baby Jesus.*

Theatrical little creature that she was, Margaret was undoubtedly much attracted to the church's aura of theater and mysticism. The Church of England, founded in defiance of Catholicism, has almost as much pomp and circumstance connected with it as does the Catholic Church. Margaret was expected to take an interest in religious affairs, anyhow, since the head of the monarchy in Britain is also the head of the Church. For Margaret and Elizabeth, that meant being immersed in religious heraldry, in an atmosphere of religion that was inseparable from their royal standing.

Although sometimes a little hellion, Margaret could also be the perfect lady. Neither pose was false. She was both adorable and impossible. And she was never malicious or unfeeling. On the contrary, she had a good heart and was a genuinely sweet and caring little girl.

Sir James Barrie, the author of *Peter Pan*, was tremendously impressed with the manner in which Margaret's decency and gentility manifested itself as early as her third birthday. There was a grand, smashing party for that occasion, and the distinguished playwright found himself seated next to the guest of honor at mealtime.

The little hostess was having the time of her life and had already opened up all her gifts and put her very favorite present next to her plate.

"Is that really your very own?" asked Barrie in mock envy.

Quick as could be, the tiny girl reached over and placed the gift between both their places. "It is yours and mine," she informed Barrie graciously.

Sir James never forgot the remark, which he later incorporated into one of his plays, and Margaret certainly never forgot Sir James, who had bowled her over with his charm. They became great chums, and later, when little Margaret heard someone speaking of Sir James Barrie, she interjected, "I know that man. He is my greatest friend and I am his greatest friend."

Although Lilibet had more plain common sense, Margaret herself wasn't lacking in practicality. Sometimes she was deucedly clever about the most esoteric things. For instance, at yet another children's party, where a magician performed, Margaret replied with the greatest of sense when she was urged to take a seat in the very front row. She demurred accepting the greater proximity to the conjurer. "No, thank you," she said politely. "I shall see *too well*." She then gratefully accepted a place farther back.

The lives of the two sisters were drastically changed by that one event which so greatly altered the history of the world and which made them the beloved Little Princesses as well—the abdication of their Uncle David shortly before his scheduled coronation as King Edward VIII. Bertie never coveted the throne. He never wished to be king; he dreaded the limelight. And his wife wanted it even less.

Yet what could be done about the dreadful matter? During the period between the death of his father, George V, and his eventual abdication, David, as King Edward VIII, did little other than cause grief in the higher circles of British government.

The populace, thanks to the voluntary censorship by English newspapers, knew practically nothing of Edward VIII's affair with the twice-wed American socialite. The romance that was being treated as front page news in Wallis's own country was being hushed up by Fleet Street while steps were being taken to prevent a total Parliamentary crisis.

Theories regarding what might have

happened—had Prime Minister Stanley Baldwin not pushed Edward VIII out of the throne and the country—abound. But who could say today how things might have been? We can deal only with what actually happened there and then and with the genuine sentiments in England at that time. Amongst the higher-ups in Parliament the ruling sentiment was that, regardless of Wallis Warfield Simpson, Edward VIII wasn't what Britons needed to guide their country.

The situation between Mrs. Simpson and David Windsor, in retrospect, appears to have been almost fated. There was no other end in sight for him, than abdication. Though the sophisticated divorcée was willing to give up the king so he could continue to rule his country, he wouldn't hear of it for a moment. He wasn't willing to go on without the woman he loved. So he managed to convince himself that he would be allowed to marry Mrs. Simpson and make her his queen. It was a most fantastic pipe dream.

The thought of accepting Mrs. Simpson as queen was abhorrent to Parliament, especially to Baldwin, who considered the fact that Edward VIII was king trouble enough. Baldwin at last informed the monarch that there would be no place for Mrs. Simpson as queen consort, nor even as the king's wife through the compromise situation of a morganatic marriage.

Interestingly enough, one of the persons most opposed to the king's marriage had a morganatic marriage in her own background. Queen Mary's grandfather, Duke Alexander of Württemberg, had wed morganatically. But Queen Mary couldn't bear the thought of her son marrying Mrs. Simpson. She refused again and again to even meet the woman.

And so Edward VIII was given his ultimatum—renounce Mrs. Simpson or be prepared for a total crisis of government in the face of Parliament stepping down.

At last the king forced himself to accept the unhappy truth. Mrs. Simpson could never be his queen. As his wife, she could perhaps be accepted by most of his subjects, but the crisis of Parliament that would come in the wake of such a marriage would be difficult, if not impossible, to resolve.

In addition to the issue of Mrs. Simpson, the king knew many people were having other thoughts—thoughts about what a fine ruler his brother Albert would be. The general consensus was that his steady, reliable younger brother was preferable as king. He made his decision after much consideration of his own future and of his country's. He decided to step down from the throne, so that his brother Albert, the duke of York, could take his place.

It was this event, so far from their understanding at the time, that was to so greatly change the lives of Elizabeth and Margaret. Both girls adored their Uncle David. Neither had met Mrs. Simpson during this period, though she had once come to call on their mother. Margaret, ever the dramatic romanticist, didn't understand what all this abdication business was about. She was only six, and such things as the ruling of Britannia were still quite beyond her, but she was perceptive enough to realize something quite dire was afoot. "Are they going to chop off his head?" she asked, wide-eyed, upon hearing news of Edward VIII's abdication.

When Lilibet and Margaret finally began to realize what all the fuss was about and to grasp the fact that their beloved papa was going to be king of England, they were just about as thrilled as their parents at the prospect of their new life. Which is to say, not thrilled at all.

"Just think," Margaret complained, "I've just learnt how to spell 'York'—Y-O-R-K—and now I'm not to use it anymore. I'm to sign myself Margaret, all alone."

Nor was the idea of living in Buckingham Palace terribly inviting. "You mean we've got to leave our own house?" Margaret wailed, very much perturbed. Even the usually unruffled Lilibet hated the idea of having to leave 145 Piccadilly. She suggested digging an underground tunnel between Buckingham Palace and the Royal Lodge at Windsor, so they could at least sneak back to one of the places they called "home" to sleep.

But the wheels of history cannot be controlled by little girls, and nothing Lilibet or Margaret could do or hope would change that final, fateful conversation between the king and Prime

Minister Baldwin in which Edward VIII had finally asked, "Will my marriage be approved?" Baldwin shook his head and replied, "Not by the country, sir."

Edward VIII's words at that time sealed the fate of Lilibet and Margaret, as well as his own. "I want you to be the first to know that I have made up my mind and nothing will alter it. I mean to abdicate and to marry Mrs. Simpson."

And so Lilibet and Margaret were to find themselves within the sprawling confines of Buckingham Palace, where Lilibet would comment, drily and without enthusiasm, "People who live here should have bicycles."

It was very difficult for both the girls. They couldn't understand the intricacies involved in their father's taking the throne. They had been happy at 145 Piccadilly. They had loved that house and their lives there. Unconsciously, both realized that Papa would be busier and more occupied in the days to come, with less time for them. They weren't certain of what being king consisted, but they knew that both their parents would be in their company less and less in the future.

The circumstances surrounding accession to the sovereign's position weren't joyous, nor was the family's reaction to the news that Bertie would be king. The duchess was reportedly in tears when she learned the news. Not until the actual coronation months later did any of the Yorks display happiness with their new positions in life.

By that time they had stoically accepted their duty as part of the royal family.

The stolid, shy Albert was deeply disturbed at this turn of events, even though he had seen it coming for some time. It's doubtful Bertie could ever have become the fine ruler he did without the support, every step of the way, of his lovely and capable spouse. If he had been considering finding the perfect future queen consort for his bride, he couldn't have chosen better than Elizabeth Bowes-Lyon.

One thing Elizabeth did as far back as 1926 was to make contact with a speech therapist for her husband. She saw no reason why Bertie should continue to be made so unhappy and ill at ease because of his speech impediment. It was Elizabeth who set up Bertie's first appointment with the speech therapist Lionel Logue, a renowned Australian with a practice in Harley Street.

Logue did wonders for the duke of York, who continued seeing him for several years and who was soon able, under Logue's tutelage, to make public speeches without his humiliating stammering.

It was Logue who helped Bertie prepare his coronation speech. It was Logue and Elizabeth who carefully rehearsed with him until he could deliver it with nary a stutter. It was Elizabeth who was always there to help him no matter what his problem. It was Elizabeth of whom he confided to a friend, "Elizabeth could make a home anywhere." She was probably the best thing ever to happen to him, and Bertie knew that better than anyone else.

The children helped also. The new king was deeply touched by their action the day he returned home from his accession council at St. James Palace. Coached by their governess Miss Crawford, Lilibet and Margaret knew now that their papa had just been officially made king. When he walked through the front door, the two little ones rushed to him, then halted suddenly and dropped down into two demure curtsies. The new monarch was profoundly moved by this gesture of respect from his very favorite subjects!

The coronation was, of course, an amazingly involved procedure, especially with two children taking part in it. There was much more to be learned and absorbed than simple curtsies. This was one of the major events of England in decades, especially since Edward VIII hadn't remained the ruler long enough to have *his* coronation. That meant it was the first ceremony of its kind since George V succeeded to the throne in 1910. After twenty-six years, England was ready for a very stirring, extravagant ceremonial.

It was decided that Albert should take the name of his late father in assuming the crown, thereby becoming King George VI. The reasons behind this involved little more than good public relations, which should never be underrated. The people of Great Britain had been through a confusing crisis with the abdication. Edward

VIII, while glumly regarded by British politicians, had been a warm, gay, fun-loving monarch, much beloved by the British public. Naturally, Albert's advisors were concerned about how the people would react to him as their new king.

Speech impediment aside, Bertie was also considered just plain unexciting. Now, after Edward VIII's short but tumultuous rule, it was felt that a good dose of dullness was just what the folks needed. After all, hadn't Britons ended up adoring the stodgy George V and his unexciting Mary, known far and wide as the least vivacious monarchs of modern time? In point of fact, George V and his spouse were considered so boring that Max Beerbohm, during their reign, circulated a daring little ditty to just that effect—an imaginary argument, in the form of a ballad, as to just which one was the duller, George or Mary.

And now, here was Bertie, a far cry from his *bon vivant*, café society elder brother, having to take his place in the eyes of the public and, hopefully, in their hearts as well.

Bertie may have been shy and stammering, but he was also responsible, kind and dependable. He had all those fine qualities Queen Mary had pointed out to Elizabeth Bowes-Lyon, which were just as important in a husband as they were in a king. Bertie was a far cry from being a flashy intellectual show-off (not that anyone would have termed David Windsor a genius), but the fact that Bertie had finished 68th in his class of 68 at Osborne was not as important as the fact that he was a good man and a benevolent man.

As far as his advisors were concerned, one of the most unfortunate aspects of Albert was not his tepid personality but his name. Albert to the British would always be associated with the not particularly adored prince consort to Queen Victoria, Albert of Saxe-Coburg-Gotha.

Victoria had, of course, worshipped the ground her Albert walked upon. But she had been just about the only one. And not only had he been unloved by the populace of Great Britain, he had also been German. By 1936, when Albert, duke of York, learned he would accede to the throne, anti-German sentiment was well on the rise. It was best, his advisors felt, not to call too much attention to the memory of the prince consort, nor to the fact that the House of Hanover, from which Bertie was descended, was so Germanic that Queen Victoria herself had German blood.

So it was decided that the new king should take his father's name, carrying on the idea of stability that the country so badly needed at that time. And there was no man who had been more stable than George V. All hoped this would ease the pain of the last unhappy days of the reign of Edward VIII.

So there were Margaret and Lilibet, not only having to forget their own last name of York, but now having to remember a new name for Papa as well! It was quite confusing for two young children.

Although there were many drawbacks to Papa's being king, there were some consolations.

Both girls were tremendously excited at the prospect of the upcoming coronation, and Margaret especially looked forward to it with ever-burgeoning enthusiasm. As usual, she knew what she wanted right from the start. When her mother informed designer Norman Hartnell, within Margaret's hearing, that a train wasn't needed on Margaret's gown, just on Lilibet's, her voice piped up immediately. She *must* have a train, just like Mummy's and Lilibet's. Naturally, Margaret got a train on her gown.

Margaret might have been tremendously confident that she would do well at the coronation, but Lilibet wasn't so assured about the matter. She didn't worry about herself. No, Lilibet never did. But she did worry greatly about Margaret and she confided her fears to their governess. "I do hope she won't disgrace us all by falling asleep in the middle, Crawfie," she fretted. "After all, she is very young for a coronation, isn't she?"

Margaret was awfully young for the ceremony, but she did manage to behave herself beautifully. Afterwards, Princess Elizabeth was happy to confess that her worries over little Margaret had been needless. "She was wonderful, Crawfie!" Lilibet enthused. "I only had to nudge her once or twice when she played with the prayer books too loudly."

Margaret *was* wonderful during the coronation, which took place on May 12, 1936. She positively shone. In a way, this was Margaret's very special day in the sun, because it was the day the public fell totally in love with her. She practically stole the show, sitting on a special seat in the royal coronation carriage that was built up to a viewing level for the crowd, and waving her little hand to a cheering public. And who, of those who watched, can ever forget the sight of the new royal family on the balcony at Buckingham Palace, with the pintsized princesses, in robes and tiaras, waving and smiling and basking in all the attention being showered upon themselves and their parents? The era of the beloved Little Princesses was beginning, an era that would endear the two girls to everyone.

And those would be happy days indeed, happier than the ones that caused Britain's new queen to proclaim, as 1936 drew to a close, "Thank God this sad year is over!"

Chapter Four

Margaret easily became the darling of the public and the press. In fact, she was a press agent's dream, oozing with verve and personality. Strong-willed, teasing, mischievous, temperamental, she was feisty and fiery as only a female born under the sign of Leo could be.

As a child, Margaret already reacted adversely to not getting her own way. She was known for flinging books and other missiles about the palace during fits of pique. She was a real little Tartar.

Luckily, Margaret had Lilibet, who watched over her with infinite patience. When Miss Crawford wasn't around to mind Margaret's manners, it was Lilibet who voluntarily took over the job. This opportunity arose again and again.

Once, after a Buckingham Palace garden party, the big sister lectured the little one, "If you see anyone in a funny hat, don't laugh and point. And you mustn't be in such a hurry to reach the tea table. That's not polite, either."

There were times, of course, when even Lilibet would lose her composure. More than once, when her sister started a fight with her, the elder princess would cry, "Margaret always wants everything I want!"

It was true. Margaret did want to live by exactly the same set of rules and regulations as her sister, regardless of the four-year difference in their ages. This was her cross to bear throughout childhood. Lilibet was, after all, her senior and entitled to certain special privileges, like a half-hour-later bedtime. Margaret knew it was out of her control, but that never stopped her from protesting.

Margaret's worries about being left out were only increased when her father became king. That step made Elizabeth heiress presumptive to the British throne and meant that she would get all sorts of special attention. This situation was never easy for Margaret to handle, but even worse was that Elizabeth's position also meant she'd be getting the undivided attention of Papa. Perhaps that was the most difficult reality for Margaret to face.

In all honesty, however, Margaret fared quite well during her early childhood. She was noted and loved for her cheery disposition and liveliness. Some of that charm could be quite calculated, as when the irresistible princess would cajole adults out of being angry with her by gaily singing "Who's Afraid of the Big Bad Wolf?" But at other times, the majority of times, Margaret was captivatingly guileless, winningly sincere. One such time was the evening her nanny assured her that nothing was impossible if one tried hard enough. "Oh, Alah," she disagreed knowingly, "have you ever tried putting the toothpaste back into the tube?"

Then, too, there were times when her loving ways would leave not a dry eye in the house. When the little pony Peggy died, rather than mope about, Margaret assured everyone with utmost childlike confidence, "Now I expect Jesus is riding her, instead of that silly old donkey."

Of course, Margaret and Lilibet were sheltered during their early years, and there was nary a chance they might have led anything approaching a normal childhood. Today, this has been changed. Elizabeth's own children have attended British schools and followed a regime more typical of other upper-class youngsters. But during the reign of George VI, the monarchy was still much more removed from the general public.

Lilibet and Margaret never attended a school, never tasted of the "normal" life, never had a gaggle of girlfriends with whom to pass the time. All their lessons were private. There was Miss Crawford for their general studies, which consisted of literature, English history and the like.

There was Miss Vacani for their private dancing classes, Miss Daly for swimming, and Horace Smith to teach them riding. As for group lessons with other children their own age, there were none.

It was rather a lonely childhood. Bertie was a very busy man, especially after he'd acceded to the throne. He was also not demonstrative with his children. It was a simple thing, though, for little Margaret to melt Bertie's composure and reduce him to happy smiles. But it was Lilibet to whom he gave most of his time. He was a man who considered devotion to duty his highest responsibility. His daughter Elizabeth was going to be queen one day, and he didn't want to leave her in the same position in which his father had left him—ignorant of the workings of the British government.

Besides the king's natural sense of duty towards Lilibet, he was also drawn to her because she shared his tastes far more than did Margaret, who always remained so like her Uncle David. Lilibet loved to go riding with Papa, and when she was old enough to shoot, she took that up as well. Margaret was much happier watching the television or being taken to see a play.

The queen was an adoring mother and a reluctant ruler. She regretted the time spent away from the girls, at social events, on official business, often on trips of lengthy duration. But she, too, felt the call of duty and was often forced to put her country before her family.

Adding to the stress of duty was the queen's frail health. She was often abed with a virus or influenza (she had even been taken ill on her honeymoon) which kept her from her daughters. With no other children their own age around—other than an occasional and welcomed visit from one young cousin or another—Lilibet and Margaret naturally fell into spending most of their time together. They grew closer than most sisters their age. If they hadn't, they would have been lonelier still.

Margaret never sensed that she and her big sister were anything but equals—at least amongst themselves. She loved playing with Lilibet by the hour in their tiny Welsh cottage, practicing the very unprincessly chores of cooking and cleaning. "We've got everything except a telephone," Margaret once boasted proudly of their little house. Whenever the family was at the Lodge in Windsor, the children could be found in their little house, acting out a lifestyle that had more to do with middle-class, mundane preoccupations than with the trappings of royalty.

The Little Princesses truly had a special closeness and love for each other, but their childhood was also marked by competitiveness, certainly on Margaret's part. The fact that Elizabeth received different treatment never failed to irk Margaret during her childhood or in later years. "I was born too late!" wailed the Littlest Princess, the Imperfect One, in anger at the privileges bestowed by fate upon her older sister.

As in most cases of sibling rivalry, Margaret's envy spurred her on to pranks of childish spite. Whenever she was feeling slightly neglected, Margaret evened the score by dropping salt in her sister's tea or dumping tapioca in her bathwater. When Lilibet was puffed with understandable pride after having won a certificate for lifesaving skills, Margaret, not taking this lightly, wreaked havoc on a Buckingham Palace garden party by hurling Lilibet's pet Corgi into the pond and then diving in to "rescue" him. As she clambered from the water, sodden and dripping in her best party frock, Margaret's face was a study in triumph. She was a very resourceful child.

Margaret Rose meant well, but for some reason she just hadn't inherited her parents' sense of diligence and responsibility. Lilibet seemed to have gotten the full measure of those qualities.

Still, Margaret never ceased trying to do her part. Once, when Lilibet had set out a neat and orderly garden of daffodils and tulips, Margaret decided she should experiment with the horticulture route herself. So she planted row upon row of potatoes, working industriously until they were all in the ground. But patience was never among her virtues, and her usual inability to sit back and allow things to take their course got in the way. Before the potatoes had had half a chance to grow, Margaret was pulling them all up one by one to see how they were doing! She could never stand waiting or being kept in the dark about anything, even if it meant ending up defeating her own efforts.

Margaret showed little interest in Corgis for her pets. Always the shocker, she chose a toad and a salamander instead. At the early age of ten, she managed to shock even her generally unperturbable sister, when she remarked to Lilibet that she considered the footmen at the palace a handsome lot. The prim and proper Lilibet was mortified at Margaret's raciness.

Though she exalted in making trouble at times, Margaret would be crushed at others when she would realize that her family were quietly throwing up their hands at her wild behavior. She was, beneath all her misbehaving, eager to please and to be accepted and loved as a good girl. It was this need for acceptance that spurred her to rush to her mother, when the king and queen were returning from a trip to the United States, with her pleased claim, "Look, Mummy! I am quite a good shape now, not like a football like I used to be."

Margaret's love of the artistic side of life, of music and plays and television and movies, never kept her from being interested as well in government and the ruling of her country. She was always a voracious reader and was fascinated by the machinations of history. Her active mind never ceased to notice and question things. One day she totally startled Miss Crawford by asking,

"What is the Regency Act?"

After receiving Miss Crawford's detailed explanation, seven-year-old Margaret sagely nodded. "I see," she stated concisely. "A regent is in lieu of the king." Crawfie was amazed that the princess had managed to condense the explanation into the most concise definition possible.

Margaret's interest in government helped her understand and even appreciate the fact that Lilibet would one day rule as queen while she, Margaret, had little chance of wearing the crown. And, even as a tot, she was aware that Lilibet possessed all the solid qualities needed to rule the empire—qualities in which she, Margaret, was somewhat lacking.

Once, after a lecture from her mother on some misbehavior, Margaret remarked wisely, "Isn't it lucky that Lilibet's the elder?"

Chapter Five

One thing Margaret was never unaware of
when she was growing up was her right and desire
to have a good time. It's typical of Margaret that
she reacted to the news of World War II with her
usual fury at anything which interfered with her
own life and plans.

She was nine when war broke out in Poland.
The family had been planning a holiday at
Balmoral. Now the king decided he must cancel
the proposed trip, realizing the urgent necessity of
his staying in London. Little Margaret didn't like
that at all. "Who *is* this Hitler, spoiling everything?" she stormed angrily. He had ruined her
holiday, and that was enough to make Margaret a
sworn enemy of the Fuehrer.

The real facts of the war were beyond the

comprehension of such a young child. She couldn't understand the nonaggression pact between Germany and Russia which Hitler announced in August of 1939; she couldn't understand his unleashing his troops in Poland in September, overtly challenging Britain's guarantee against foreign aggression to that country. And Margaret certainly couldn't understand the full impact of the speech made by Neville Chamberlain, the prime minister of Great Britain, broadcast to the world on the morning of Sunday, September 3.

"I am speaking to you from the Cabinet Room at Number 10 Downing Street," he said sadly at that time. "This morning, the British Ambassador in Berlin handed the German government a final note, stating that unless the British government heard from them by 11 A.M. that they were prepared at once to withdraw troops from Poland, a state of war would exist between us."

The prime minister, his hopes for "peace in our time" now a futile farce, paused before continuing his grave announcement. "I have to tell you now," he went on, "that no news of such undertaking has been received and consequently this country is at war with Germany."

That was in the morning. By evening, King George VI was on the radio speaking to his subjects, delivering slowly but without stammering, a speech he had prepared and rehearsed that very same day with the help of his wife.

"In this grave hour," he stated quietly, "perhaps in the most fateful in our history, I send to every household of my people, both at home and overseas, this message. . . . For the sake of all that we ourselves hold dear, and of the world's peace and order, it is unthinkable that we should refuse to meet this challenge. . . . To this high purpose, I now call my people at home and my people across the seas. I ask them to stand firm and united in this time of trial."

In a certain sense, the dreaded war caused the House of Windsor to stand firm and united once again. The duke of Windsor, the former King Edward VIII, returned to London from his voluntary exile, anxious to do his part in the war effort. David hadn't had much contact with his brother Bertie since he had chosen to abdicate. This was considered by many to be the doing of David's sister-in-law Elizabeth, who never did have any use for those who weren't willing to give their all for duty's sake.

Now, the duke of Windsor was warmly received by the king and appointed to the British Military Mission in Paris. This post didn't work out, however. There was a great risk of the duke's being kidnapped by the Germans as long as he remained in France. Though he was willing to give up his life for his country, there was more than David's wishes to consider. If he were taken captive by the Germans, it could destroy the British war effort. So George VI gave his elder brother a new position, one he held until 1947.

David Windsor was made governor of the Bahamas.

During the war, Lilibet, as usual, gave little thought to herself and much to her sister Margaret. She did her best to shield Margaret and to keep any disturbing news away from her. Once, after hearing grownups discussing frightening war news within earshot of Margaret, Lilibet chided them. "I don't think people should talk about battles in front of Margaret," she cautioned. "We don't want to upset her."

The queen made certain her daughters were as safe as they could be, keeping them in Scotland or at Windsor for the duration of the war. But she could not heed Neville Chamberlain's advice and send them to Canada, where they would be out of danger completely.

"The children could not go without me," she matter-of-factly explained, "and I could not possibly leave the king."

And so the queen sent her two daughters out of London—first to Birkhall and then to the Royal Lodge at Windsor. At last, when the bombings grew worse and fell closer to Windsor, the queen had her daughters installed, along with their governess and a small staff, in the heavily fortified Windsor Castle itself.

Little Margaret worried a great deal about her mother and father. When her parents had to leave Birkhall in 1939 and return to London because of Chamberlain's announcement of war, she had anxiously asked, "Why had Mummy and Papa to go back to London? Will the Germans come and get them?"

Even after being assured that her Mummy and Papa were in no immediate danger of being carried off by the Germans, Margaret couldn't rest in peace. The king and queen telephoned at 6 P.M. each evening from London, and Margaret was always the most eager to speak with them. She always wanted to reassure herself that they were alive and well. All the protectiveness in the world couldn't keep some of the harsh reality of war from the child.

The war wasn't a strictly grim affair for the two girls, however. Like everyone else, they had their moments of fun and happiness. Margaret was nearly ten when the war began and within a week of being fifteen when it ended, she practically grew up during World War II and it constituted an important part of her childhood.

With the buoyant, lively spirit that was so much a part of her, Margaret was determined to triumph over the despair and hardship of the Second World War. She refused to let it get the best of her.

Margaret threw herself into "appreciating" the war with a vengeance. She became a "fan" of the air battles and adored watching the flares and smoke in the sky. She just wouldn't dwell in the death and danger lurking behind the sky-show facade. With Lilibet, she watched part of the Battle of Britain from the doorway of the summerhouse at the Home Park in Windsor, and, true little actress that she was, she was enthralled by the drama.

While they were at Windsor, the princesses were allowed to play in the park there, but they were well protected and always under heavy surveillance. Whenever a warning of "enemy aircraft overhead" was given, an armored tank would speed to their playing area to rush them safely back home. Margaret was always the last to get inside the tank, always attempting to steal one final peek at the hostilities, at the approaching, swooping planes, before being taken away.

At Windsor, the girls were prepared for the worst, though it was infrequent that they had to head down below to the air raid shelters. When they did, they clutched dainty overnight bags, kept packed and ready for any emergency.

In the family tradition, the girls were filled with patriotism and always bursting with pride over their Mummy and Papa's efforts. As expected, their duty-devoted mother would allow no shirkers in the family. She sent word to the staff at Windsor that Margaret and Lilibet were under no circumstances to eat any more than the official quota of sweets. And at home, in Buckingham Palace, she made equally certain that rationing was constantly adhered to. She would not allow anyone to treat herself, her husband or her children differently from other Britons.

The king and queen didn't hide in fortified castles during the war, either. They were always out on the streets, mingling with their subjects, witnessing firsthand the sacrifices and suffering of the common people. The queen felt she was doing no more than her part when she observed quotas, when she shunned visits to the dressmakers, when she kept her daughters in altered versions of last year's clothes. Neither Elizabeth nor Bertie was the type to take advantage of their own position of power and privilege to get more than their share of allotted goods. They were in this war on the same basis as other Britons.

The war years had few easy days. The king and queen were shattered when enemy aircraft dropped bombs on their former home, totally destroying 145 Piccadilly. They were heartbroken when their friend and favorite actor Leslie Howard was killed. In a bizarre turn of events, his civilian plane was shot down over the Bay of Biscay. For some time rumor had it that the plane had been shot at only because the Germans had been misinformed and told King George VI would be on board. Perhaps the most personally grievous incident of the war came in 1942, when the king was informed that his younger brother George, the duke of Kent, had been killed. The duke, an air commodore in the RAF, was killed when his Sunderland Flying Boat crashed in Scotland during a routine flight.

Still, the indomitable spirits of Bertie and Elizabeth, though dashed and sometimes flagging, could not be defeated. In March of 1939, the queen showed her valor beautifully when she addressed the women of the United States in a memorable speech.

The Lend-Lease Act had just been passed by the United States, helping to give Britain millions of dollars worth of arms for the fight against the Germans. Now the queen, forgetting her own deprivation and suffering, made a speech filled with hope and gratitude.

"Wherever I go," she said, "I see bright eyes and smiling faces, for though our road is stony and hard, it is straight and we know that we fight in a good cause. The warmth and sympathy of American generosity has touched beyond measure the hearts of all of us living and fighting in these islands. It has given us strength to know that you have not been content to pass us by on the other side. To us in the time of our tribulations, you have surely shown that compassion which has been for two thousand years the mark of the good neighbor. We shall not forget your sacrifice."

Her own sacrifice was not small. She attended six public engagements each week, a great many for any person, an astounding tally for a woman who preferred remaining out of the public eye. She gladly sacrificed her home life for the time being, because it was for that life Britain was fighting.

During yet another speech, the queen reminded British women, "It is, after all, for our homes and for their security that we are fighting and we must see to it that, despite all the difficulties of these days, our homes do not lose those very qualities which make them the background as well as the joy of our lives."

On Friday, September 13, 1940, at 11 A.M., the truth of the war was brought close to home for the king and queen. Elizabeth and Bertie were working in a small sitting room at Buckingham Palace when the drone of an airplane broke the quiet. They looked up to a vision from their worst nightmares—a lone German bomber was tearing straight over the mall, heading right for them.

Thinking quickly, the king pulled the queen to the floor, away from the windows, as they heard the first of several bombs come crashing down on the palace. Later, they were informed that, if not for Bertie's quick thinking, both of them could have been seriously injured by glass flying from the breaking windows.

Luckily, there was no bodily harm done to either of the monarchs, though the bomber had scored several direct hits on the palace itself. Bertie and Elizabeth were both shaken up by the raid, though not so much that the queen couldn't smile appreciatively when one of the palace policemen saluted her and grinningly remarked, "A magnificent piece of bombing, Ma'am, if you'll pardon my saying so." It would take more than a world war to dampen the dry British sense of humor.

Later, the queen admitted she wasn't all that dismayed to have been a target and to have had bombs crashing into the palace, not when she thought about some of the full-scale disaster areas of London. "I'm glad we've been bombed," she explained. "It makes me feel I can look the East End in the face."

Buckingham Palace was bombed a total of nine times during the war. None of this ever caused the king and queen to shirk what they considered their duties as British subjects and as British rulers.

Even little Margaret began to display a devotion to duty that did the family proud. She diligently spent hour upon hour knitting a little wool scarf to be put on display for Queen Mary's London Needlework Guild. And, of course, she played her own small but important role in Lilibet's famous Children's Hour broadcast.

It was during the height of the Battle of Britain that Lilibet herself came up with the idea. The princess suggested she go on the radio for the Children's Hour, at 5 P.M., to speak to the children of Great Britain, sending a message of cheer and support. The king was touched and pleased, and he told his daughter he thought it was a splendid idea.

Naturally, Margaret wanted to get into the act as well. She certainly didn't want to miss out on *this*. Her sympathetic big sister told her not to worry and promised there would be a spot for her on the broadcast as well.

And so Lilibet's voice, already strong and resonant, rang out across the airwaves of the world. "All we children at home are full of cheerfulness and courage..." she said. "We know, every one of us, that in the end, all will be well." And then, as she ended her affecting speech, she added, "My sister is by my side and we are both going to say goodnight to you. Come on, Margaret."

And there couldn't have been a finish more tender than the sound of Margaret's sweet little voice joining in to say, "Good night and good luck to you all." Even today, with the Second World War a period for vague nostalgia, the Children's Hour broadcast of Princess Elizabeth and Princess Margaret is remembered by all who heard it with heartfelt affection.

It was only in keeping with their background and upbringing that the two Little Princesses should have felt this devotion to the call of duty, this responsibility towards the other citizens of their country. From the day she had become queen, their mother had been telling them, "Your work is the rent you pay for the room you occupy on earth." And they were never allowed to forget the whys and wherefores of the proper behavior of royalty.

Margaret, though, wanted to be as much like other girls as possible. And if she couldn't have all the things that regular girls had—school chums, trips to the zoo, the cinema and other public places, in short, freedom—then she was going to make darned sure she got as many as she could!

It was Margaret's nudging for "normal" privileges as opposed to those of the royal variety that led to one of the most interesting episodes of the girls' childhoods. Margaret loved to stage plays as a child, and she would spend hours off by herself sketching stage sets and designing extremely sophisticated costumes for theatricals she wished she could present. Since Margaret loved show business so much, it was inevitable that sooner or later she would be allowed to put on a production.

It was during the war that Margaret, bored at being stuck up at Windsor with so little to do (except for such brief respites as a welcome holiday at Balmoral with Mummy and Papa in 1941, when the Germans were busily occupied on the Russian front), came up with the idea of presenting some plays herself, with all proceeds to benefit the queen's Wool Fund.

At first, Margaret's plan met with little enthusiasm on the home front. But at last the adults gave in. These plays, they reasoned, could do no harm. Margaret and Lilibet could be kept happily occupied, and money for a worthwhile cause would be raised as well.

To that end, several plays were produced at Windsor. Margaret and Lilibet did the sets, and Margaret designed most of the costumes. Margaret was always cast in the principal female role and Elizabeth always played the principal male. There were always several other children of nobility in smaller parts. In 1941, the sisters starred in *Cinderella*; in 1942, it was *The Sleeping*

Beauty; 1943 brought *Aladdin*; and in 1944, the girls put on their final production, *Old Mother Red Riding Boots*.

Right from the word go, little Margaret knew the venture would be a financial success, and it was. It wasn't Margaret's style to doubt her ability as a crowd-pleaser. Once, when costs were being discussed, she predicted in airy confidence, "They'll pay anything to see us." A bit blunt for a pubescent member of royalty, perhaps, but Margaret knew what she was talking about, as several hefty deposits to the Wool Fund proved.

What Margaret wanted most during her childhood, war or no war, was to have a good time. When she was being allowed to have her fun, she could be a perfect angel. Crossed, she became a pintsized virago.

"Who is this Hitler, spoiling everything?" Margaret had asked when the war began. And she never forgot her grudge. When news finally came that the war in Europe had ended, Margaret's reaction was to immediately hurl her German books to the floor, declaring on the spot her intention to never learn another word of that horrid Hitler's language.

And then, on Sunday, May 6, 1945, the war truly ended for the Little Princesses. With the king and queen, they left Windsor and returned to London. Perhaps they hadn't been overly fond of Buckingham Palace when they had originally taken residence there. But now it was different. Now it looked like home.

Chapter Six

After the war, Elizabeth and Margaret entered what could be termed the most normal period of their lives. These were halcyon days, with everyone glad that peace had come and with the entire royal family feeling tremendously thankful and pleased to be together at home once again. These days were the magical ones, the blissful ones that once led Margaret to avow, "I cannot imagine anything more wonderful than to be who I am."

This was also the period of least competitiveness between Margaret and Lilibet. The two had had their jealous moments (or, to be precise, Margaret had had hers) during the war years, especially when Elizabeth turned sixteen and registered for national service. Her little sister was still, of course, far too young to take part.

Poor Margaret! She sometimes thought life meant always being left out. She was a furious twelve-year-old when her father appointed Lilibet a colonel in the Grenadier Guards. She was even angrier when Lilibet followed that up by joining the Auxiliary Territorial Service in 1945. Was Margaret never to be allowed to take part?

As it turned out, Lilibet's being in A.T.S. wasn't all that hard to take. She received no special treatment, being listed officially simply as "No. 230873, Second Subaltern Elizabeth Alexandra Mary Windsor." And so, at eighteen, Elizabeth was learning how to drive an army lorry and do vehicle repairs—certainly not glamorous jobs. Margaret ended up not even being terribly bitter about being too young to join up. And one aspect of the situation gave the younger sister great satisfaction. That was Lilibet's terribly unflattering A.T.S. uniform. It was cold comfort, perhaps, but to always-left-out Margaret, it was comfort enough.

Everyone, especially big sister Elizabeth, continued to do whatever they could to make Margaret a part of things, but the fact remained that she *was* four years Lilibet's junior, and those four years were going to make a big difference whether Margaret liked it or not.

Elizabeth did try very hard to make sure her younger sister was included whenever possible. For instance, when she joined the Girl Guides, Lilibet did everything in her power to convince Miss Violet Synge, the guide commissioner, to allow her younger sister to join, even though she was well aware that Margaret was, by rights, too young.

"You don't think you could get her in somehow?" she prodded Mrs. Synge. "She is very strong, you know. Pull up your skirts, Margaret," she prompted, "and show Miss Synge. You can't say those aren't a very fine pair of hiking legs, Miss Synge. And she loves getting dirty, don't you, Margaret? And how she would love to cook sausages on sticks."

Lilibet got her way, of course. Such determination was bound to pay off. Margaret was deemed too young to be a Girl Guide, but she was made a Brownie and allowed to share in her sister's Guiding activities.

Now, being with the Girl Guides wasn't the same for the Little Princesses as it was for most girls. There was always a threat of kidnapping to the nobility, so even at their most public, Elizabeth and Margaret were well protected and led the most sheltered of lives. Their fellow Girl Guides would arrive at Windsor Park for picnics and hikes and wienie roasts—it wasn't as if Lilibet and Margaret were allowed to go traipsing around in just *any* woods. And, ironically, the sisters were in for a jolting surprise when they had their first Guide meeting. Lilibet and Margaret were garbed in the oldest clothes, excited at the prospect of mucking about and getting grubby. Then the other girls arrived. Their parents, thrilled that their daughters were mingling with the princesses, had dressed them in frilly party frocks for the occasion! No matter how much they attempted to ignore the truth, Lilibet and Margaret weren't like other girls, and they realized it.

How many other London children would have been excited beyond measure at the mere prospect of taking the underground? For most city children, a ride on the tube was the most common of everyday experiences. Public transportation was the cheapest and simplest mode of travel. But for Margaret, the prospect of a ride on the underground was a dream come true.

The excursion wasn't announced beforehand to the public, the better to allow Margaret, Lilibet, their governess Miss Crawford, and family friend Lady Helen Graham to travel inconspicuously. The four boarded at St. James Park and took the train to Charing Cross, where they then changed trains to arrive at Tottenham Court Road.

For Margaret and Lilibet it was magical. They gazed about themselves with awe, clutching their London Transport tickets in their hands, enviously viewing their fellow passengers, to whom this was just a mundane experience.

Unfortunately, news of the princesses seated in the No Smoking car with their chaperones soon reached Fleet Street, and when their party exited at Tottenham Court Road, a bevy of cameramen were waiting for them. But it had been fun while it lasted. Several years later, Margaret would get a kick out of taking her first double-decker bus ride.

Perhaps the greatest thrill of Margaret and Lilibet's young lives came on V. E. Day. There was dancing in the streets of London that evening, as thousands upon thousand of Britishers expressed their joy at the end of hostilities in Europe. The king, knowing how much his daughters missed not being able to share in the experiences of other girls their age, gave them permission to go out and join the merriment in the streets. It was the kind of experience that, joyful as it was, other young women might have taken for granted. But not Lilibet and Margaret. For them, mingling secretly with the masses was as exciting as the end of the war.

They adored it. The cheering crowds, the joking, happy throng making their way down the Mall to Trafalgar Square and then onward to Piccadilly—it was a special night for everyone involved. Elizabeth and Margaret looked like everyone else, in their cloth coats and head-scarves, with no detectives or guards dogging their footsteps, just two pleasant young officers acting as their escorts and enjoying the celebration as much as the girls did.

Back in 1936 when he had abdicated, Edward VIII had turned to his brother and remarked, "You'll make a good king, Bertie." During the postwar years there were few who didn't consider George VI one of the finest monarchs in England's history. Much of his earlier awkwardness had disappeared, his stuttering was barely a problem anymore; he wasn't nearly as withdrawn as he had been when younger. Everyone loved Bertie all the more for his newfound confidence.

The war, along with the influence of his wife Elizabeth, had helped bring Bertie out of his shell. Mingling with his subjects became a genuine pleasure for this sensible, down-to-earth ruler. He discovered that he *enjoyed* being king, that the position he had so dreaded wasn't such a terrible burden after all.

In his forties, Bertie came into his own. His father's strict, impatient handling of his son had caused Bertie's withdrawal. George V had taught his son little about government, but much about intolerance: he would lose his temper watching Bertie's face twist from the effort of forcing out difficult syllables of speech. As long as verbalization remained such an agonizing process for Albert, his father was barely able to hear beyond the words to the thoughts being uttered. So Bertie had learned to keep quiet, to stay in the background, to keep those thoughts to himself.

Ironically, it was the events set in motion by George V's death that were to banish Bertie's awkwardness and tongue-tied social unease. Unfortunately, his father didn't live to see how well Bertie learned to cope with his speech impediment. Upon receiving the crown, Albert realized that he could no longer hang back. He was the king and he had to do his duty.

That prescription ended up being just what the doctor ordered. The George VI of the late 1940s bore little resemblance to Albert, duke of York. The new Bertie had self-confidence. He was socially gracious, but he still preferred avoiding social gatherings if possible. He was truly a happy man, with a wonderful, loving wife and two adorable daughters. His happiness touched everyone with whom he came into contact, most especially his family. And now that the war was ended, the king and queen and their daughters were really and truly a family.

King George VI continued to dote on both his girls, though they were well on the way to being young ladies and not children now. His strict grandmama, Queen Victoria, would have been aghast at his permissive attitude towards Lilibet and Margaret. "You are only young once—have a good time," he once told Margaret, and he meant every word of that advice.

Though the king and queen tried to be easygoing with their children, they didn't allow them to get away with untoward behavior or slacking of duties. They weren't strict, but they did expect a great deal from their daughters. They knew how much lay within the capabilities of both Elizabeth and Margaret, and they didn't want either of their girls to settle for less.

It's important to remember that their Majesties were never frivolous, carefree folks, although they certainly had their share of light-hearted moments. More than anything they still believed in old-fashioned virtues, they still held dear all the values which had served to make England strong.

Religion was a mainstay in the lives of everyone of the royal family, and Margaret was as ecumenically bent as the rest, if not more so. Her parents were firm believers in the will and justice of God, and their faith was always deep and powerful. The queen meant every word of it when she told a meeting of the World's Evangelical Alliance, "I can truly say that the king and I long to see the Bible back where it ought to be, as a guide and comfort in the homes and lives of our people. From our own experience, we know what the Bible can mean for personal life."

Little did the queen realize what a large part religion and her church, the Church of England, would later play in a drama that was just now germinating. Peter Townsend, a British war hero, had already entered into the royal scene. A few years later, his romance with Princess Margaret would set the British aristocracy on their collective ear and provide gossips with the juiciest fodder since Margaret's Uncle David had chucked it all for the woman he loved.

It was on August 1, 1944 that the announcement was made of Peter Townsend's arrival in the royal household. He joined under a scheme initiated by George VI whereby outstanding young heroes of the services would be rewarded by being appointed "Equerries of Honor" and given the chance to serve the king and queen in a personal capacity.

Townsend's credentials as a war hero were impressive enough. He had been born of sturdy, reliable, middle-class stock in Rangoon, where his father was a *pukka sahib* in His Majesty's Civil Service. At the age of four, Peter was brought back to England, where his family settled in the Somerset village of Crowcombe.

Peter Townsend was an average, unobtrusive child. He attended public school at Haileybury College, an institution dedicated to turning out future Indian Civil Servants. But Townsend was never to get that post in India. Like his three brothers, Peter chose a career in the armed forces instead.

He was a jesting but totally dedicated airman. In 1940, he was awarded the Distinguished Flying Cross. Soon after that, he was given a bar to add to it. In February of 1940, he led the attack and fired the bursts that brought down the first enemy plane on British soil. And yet, Townsend was carefree enough that he never failed, when passing over his hometown of Crowcombe, to slow-roll his airplane in greeting. Such were the makings of a romantic war hero.

In 1941, Townsend received the Distinguished Service Order. He was also married that year, to Cecil Rosemary Pawle, the daughter of an army brigadier. She was the perfect choice—or so it appeared at the time—for a man like Townsend.

Even at his own wedding, Townsend could make a joke about the importance of the services in his life. His career as a pilot *was* his life at that time; nothing could approach it in importance. When he and his bride left the thirteenth century church in Much Hadham after their marriage ceremony, it was to the services that Peter's mind flew. A guard of honor had been formed by the men of Townsend's squadron to line the way as he exited the building with his new wife. Peter eyed them in mock suspicion, then joked, "I hope this doesn't mean that the planes are being neglected." It was only a jest, but it showed what was most in his thoughts.

When the airman became acquainted with his king, much mutual warmth and admiration was exchanged. As a matter of fact, George VI once remarked, "If I had had a son, I'd have liked a boy like Townsend." He never for a moment suspected that, after his own death, his daughter would come close to marrying Townsend and making him a part of the royal family.

Three months after becoming an Equerry of Honor, Townsend and his wife were settled into a grace-and-favor cottage in Windsor Great Park, a secluded residence nestled behind a ten-foot privet hedge in the sprawling grounds.

The reigning monarch doted upon Townsend. In fact, it wasn't at all surprising that, when the flyer's second son was born, the king himself served as godfather. Nor was it odd that the entire royal family attended the christening. They liked the Townsends. Lilibet and Margaret were especially fond of the couple, and they took to dropping in at the cottage to visit and play with the babies whenever they had the chance.

To visit with Townsend himself, it wasn't

necessary to drop in anywhere. He was often present at the palace itself, and he was invariably the Equerry deputized to escort one or the other of the king's daughters at official functions whenever a member of the royal household was required for that service.

In 1947, Peter Townsend spent an entire three and a half months traveling with the royal family, accompanying them on their tour of South America. And he wasn't unhelpful. Calm and responsible, Townsend could assume control with ease and managed to keep everyone on schedule and well organized. When the king turned to Townsend once during this period and assured him, "I don't know what I'd do without you, Peter," he meant every word he was saying.

So vital did Townsend prove to the family that in 1950, the king promoted the Acting Group Captain (which is the equivalent of a United States colonel) to the position of Deputy Master of the Royal Household. It would still take a few years before Townsend's proximity to the royal family came close to erupting into a national crisis.

In the meantime, those postwar years had little of crisis about them. If anything, those days will be remembered for containing one of the happiest events in British history of recent times—the marriage of Princess Elizabeth to the handsome Prince of Greece, Philip Mountbatten.

To fill the office of royal son-in-law, Philip had the best of qualifications, more than just his movie-star good looks. His family had been exiled from Greece since 1922, making his title of Prince of Greece no more than a courtesy. His original name testifies to blood as Germanic as his wife's—it was Saxe-Coburg-Schleswig-Holstein Gluckstein. It was not until Philip became a naturalized British subject in 1947 that he took the surname of his uncle, Lord Mountbatten. And even *that* name was an adopted one—the original name Battenberg was metamorphosed during World War I due to anti-German hysteria.

When he married into the royal family, Philip received no dowry, but he did acquire a raft of titles. By royal decree, Philip was changed into His Royal Highness the Duke of Edinburgh, Baron Greenwich, Earl of Merioneth, and a Knight of the Garter. All that in one fell swoop!

Lilibet and Philip met back in 1939, at Dartmouth Royal Naval College. He was eighteen, she was thirteen, and it was only natural that the powers that be should decide Philip would make a nice young escort for the two princesses. They all got along well, Elizabeth and Philip especially, though they were too young for romance at the time. Then with World War II Philip was busily occupied for a few years, though he and Lilibet continued to keep in touch.

The prince and princess kept up their correspondence, and by the postwar year of 1946, they were being openly talked about as a couple.

They made an attractive twosome—the petite princess and the lanky prince. Philip's extraordinary good looks made him a public favorite right away, as did his jaunty air and the daredevil manner in which he'd tear along the Mall and through the palace gates in his little sportscar.

During Elizabeth and Philip's courtship, no one was more omnipresent than kid sister Margaret. This was a traumatic time for her, both happy and sad. She was just fourteen years old when the romance between Lilibet and Philip started blossoming, and she was fifteen when her dear sister realized she was in love with her suitor. Margaret was happy for her sister, pleased she had such a dashing beau. But at the same time, it meant feeling very left out and shoved aside again.

As a teenager, Margaret remained extremely close to her sister. Lilibet had been her best friend for as far back as she could remember. For Margaret, her closeness with Lilibet always had a degree of psychic marvelousness about it. She'd always felt that she and her sister were almost one, and she insisted they could read each other's minds. "It's no trick," she murmured one time upon finding out that she and Elizabeth were sharing the same thought. "It's telepathy. We really can do it." She wasn't the type of self-involved teenaged girl to take the loss of her sister to a man lightly.

At the same time, Margaret was agog at the idea of romantic love. Even as a child, she always seemed to have a mad crush on this fellow or that. By 1946, Margaret was such an incurable romantic that she went three times to see the

Sadlers Wells Ballet do *The Sleeping Beauty* with the lovely young Margot Fonteyn dancing the title role. It was Margaret's passion for this ballet and her admiration for the young ballerina that caused some of her friends to lightly nickname her "Margo." The name stuck and, even today, her younger relatives refer to her as "Aunt Margo."

Back in the forties, Margaret desperately wanted to be a part of the "young adult" activities of Elizabeth and Philip's crowd, and yet, as only a younger sister can, she knew perfectly well that she didn't really fit in with Lilibet's crowd anymore. A four-year gap is one thing when one child is nine and the other thirteen. But when the difference is between the ages of fourteen and eighteen, it's magnified. Lilibet had suddenly entered a grownups' world where Margaret felt gauche and out of place.

To their everlasting credit, Elizabeth and Philip did as much as they could to make certain that Margaret always felt included, even though this sometimes meant sacrificing their own privacy on their dates. Whenever they would get together at the palace to dance or play records with their friends, Margaret would be included. But she had only her string of show business impersonations and mimicked songs to offer up alongside their newfound maturity and young adulthood. Margaret couldn't help but realize that she was often more tolerated than welcomed.

Her mother sized up the situation and sought in vain for a way to rechannel Margaret's energies.

Her approach, which seemed the wisest of those open to her, was to spend more time with her younger daughter herself while at the same time being careful not to overtly discourage Margaret from keeping company with the friends of Lilibet. It saddened the queen to watch Margaret go through this difficult period of adolescence, but at the same time, she was wise enough to recognize it as a natural phase of life. The queen knew that fourteen was a difficult age for anyone and that Margaret would get through it just as every other teenager did.

Margaret adored Philip, luckily for everyone involved. This changed in later years, when she and Philip weren't always on the best of terms and when word got around the palace that he'd told her off on more than one occasion. But, back in the 1940s, she thought Lilibet was the luckiest girl on earth for having such a fabulous boyfriend. At the same time, Margaret realistically understood the problems of a royal romance—she deeply sympathized with the lack of privacy Lilibet was forced to endure as the press and public goggled at every escalation of her relationship with Philip.

A royal romance is always news, and Elizabeth and Philip's was no exception. Their steps were dogged by reporters and photographers. Their pictures were splashed across the front pages of the newspapers every day. They had little time to themselves and minimal privacy except for their time together in the palace or walking the secluded grounds at Windsor. Margaret was young, but she wasn't too young to appreciate the poignancy of a romance that had to be carried on in the public eye. "Poor Lil," she sighed early in Elizabeth's relationship with Philip. "Nothing of your own. Not even your love affair." Of course, it wouldn't be too long before Margaret would see the details of her own love story splashed across the front pages.

It was only natural that Elizabeth and Philip should think about marriage as soon as they were certain of their feelings for each other. The royal family has always been very pro-matrimony. Less than a year after Elizabeth's marriage to Philip, her mother gave a speech on the subject which could be said to sum up their Majesties' views on the state of wedlock.

The occasion was the celebration of the king and queen's silver wedding anniversary. The date, April 26, 1948, was truly a joyous one. It began with a thanksgiving service at St. Paul's Cathedral. After that, the royal pair commenced a twenty-mile car tour through the streets of London, which were lined with their loyal and loving subjects. The day ended with Queen Elizabeth speaking to the people of Great Britain on one of the subjects so dear to her heart—the importance of marriage and the importance of families staying together.

"There must be many," she suggested, "who feel as we do that the sanctities of married life are in some way the highest form of human fellowship, affording a rocklike foundation on which all the best in the life of the nation is built. Looking back over the last twenty-five years, and to my own happy childhood, I realize more and more the wonderful sense of security and happiness which comes from a loved home. Therefore at this time my heart goes out to all who are living in uncongenial surroundings, and who are longing for the time when they will have a home of their own. I am sure that patience, tolerance and love will help them to keep their faith undimmed and their courage undaunted when things seem difficult."

But, even though the king and queen greatly approved of matrimony, they didn't want daughter Elizabeth to rush into anything. They encouraged her to wait until after a trip to South Africa before deciding what to do about marriage.

The trip, to the Dominion of South Africa, in 1947, was notable in that it was Princess Margaret's first major tour. She was a rousing success. As a matter of fact, the entire royal family was a big hit with their African subjects.

The family set off for Cape Town aboard H.M.S. *Vanguard*, the largest and newest British battleship. After an enthusiastic welcome, their Majesties and the girls, accompanied by members of the staff which included Peter Townsend, journeyed across the continent, impressing their subjects at every British outpost with their poise and verve. In the meantime, Britons back home began waiting, as soon as the royal party left in

February, for their return in the spring. Everyone was eager to hear the expected engagement announcement.

They weren't disappointed. Princess Elizabeth celebrated her twenty-first birthday in South Africa. When she returned to Great Britain on May 12th, she was legally an adult and her parents were now more than happy to honor her love for Prince Philip by announcing that the two would wed. On July 10, 1947, Elizabeth's engagement became official.

The wedding, which took place on November 20, 1947, was a festive occasion, a celebration steeped in a lavishness England may never see the likes of again. The guest list was awesome and included the most impressive names in the world. There were 1,200 invited guests for the wedding, and 2,000 for the wedding banquet.

Both Elizabeth and Margaret were delicately gowned for the ceremony, wearing dresses by the "court" designer, Norman Hartnell. Though Hartnell is nowadays associated more with dowdiness than high fashion, he has had his moments, and the gowns he designed for Lilibet's wedding were among his finest creations.

Elizabeth wore a pearl-colored satin gown with a long train, while Margaret's bridesmaid's gown was of ivory silk tulle with a full, gently gathered skirt. The handsome groom, in his naval uniform, looked every bit the Prince Charming he was. The fine figure he cut had shopgirls all over Britain oohing and aahing at the princess's great luck.

An interesting sidelight to the wedding was the fact that the girls' governess, Marion Crawford, attended with her own brand-new bridegroom. She had wed Aberdeen bank manager George Buthlay shortly before Elizabeth's wedding. The press had made much of this with splashy headlines regarding Lilibet's being "beat to the altar" by Crawfie.

The pomp, circumstance and pageantry of the wedding delighted Margaret. Though their relationship wouldn't always be so smooth, she was now gratified at gaining Philip for a brother-in-law. Back in 1947, Margaret thought that Philip was swell, love was grand, and her sister deserved all the happiness in the world. Even so, she couldn't help but feel rather lonely herself.

Margaret had thrown herself into the wedding and all the preparations for it, considering every aspect of the occasion with the seriousness she felt it deserved. She spent weeks choosing what she felt was just the right wedding gift for Lilibet. She wasn't pleased until she came up with the highly original idea of giving Elizabeth and Philip a picnic set, perfect for the outdoor lifestyle the couple preferred.

Now, no sooner had the festivities ended and the newlyweds departed for a honeymoon at Birkhall than Margaret became painfully aware of her loss.

Little did Margaret realize she was about to

enter one of the most turbulent periods of her life—or that the marital happiness Elizabeth was on her way to finding was not within her own reach. It was to be a most unhappy discovery.

The rest of the family worried about Margaret's behavior during George VI's Coronation, but she was a perfect angel.

(Acme)

Little Margaret had many doting relatives to watch out for her, including her sister Lilibet and her grandmother, Queen Mary. *(Wide World Photos)*

Lucky Margaret Rose and Elizabeth! Few other children in 1933 had their own scale-sized cottage in which to play. *(Wide World Photos)*

Public appearances were sometimes fun and sometimes a bore, but were always required. *(Wide World Photos)*

The *good* part of being a princess was like a fairy tale come true. Margaret especially liked the fancy dress balls.

(Wide World Photos)

Margaret displayed her complexity while still a child. She adored putting on skits with her sister and being a Girl Guide (she's second from left in the photo) and she did her bit to help the war effort by promoting savings certificates with her sister (bottom right).

(all photos *Wide World Photos*, except upper right, *Acme*)

In their roles as Girl Guides, Lilibet and Margaret were often in the news, as when they released carrier pigeons to celebrate "Thinking Day" in Great Britain.

(Wide World Photos)

By their teens, the sisters were still inseparable in the public eye, but Margaret was already warily staring back. *(Wide World Photos)*

In 1947, a month before Lilibet wed the handsome Lieu-
tenant Philip Mountbatten, a pensive Margaret posed with
the duo. *(Wide World Photos)*

As a teenager, Margaret was already exhibiting her "Marie Antoinette aroma." At balls like this one, she was always surrounded by handsome men.

(Acme)

For her twenty-fourth birthday picture by Cecil Beaton, Margaret posed with her adored mother.

Here's the man all the fuss was about—Peter Townsend, the Group Captain who was a King's favorite, a Princess' weakness and a nation's scandal. In the lower photo, he's accompanying the Princesses on their 1947 tour of South Africa, in his role as King's Equerry.

(top photo, *U.P.I.* bottom photo, *Wide World Photos*)

The man Margaret chose to take her 29th birthday picture
was a well-known society photographer—and her new love
interest. She had fallen hard for Antony Armstrong-Jones.

Margaret's mother and other relatives had little choice about accepting her fiancé. She'd made up her mind to marry Tony, and nothing—or nobody—was going to stop her.

(Wide World Photos)

Not much over five feet tall himself, Tony was a good match for the petite princess—or so it seemed at the time.

(Wide World Photos)

The fact that she was marrying a commoner didn't mean Margaret had to settle for a less than flashy wedding. It was opulent. *(U.P.I.)*

Tony was not the ideal "royal husband." At one society ball he attended, Tony and his party were the only men, aside from the waiters, wearing black ties. *(Wide World Photos)*

At first, Tony was fascinated by the public functions he had
to attend as the husband of England's princess. It was all
new to him—and he loved it. *(Wide World Photos)*

Already showing a tendency toward dowdiness, Margaret showed up at a London cathedral for a Commonwealth Service in 1961. The next day she announced she was expecting a baby.

(Wide World Photos)

Tony had already been proclaimed Lord Snowdon. Their newborn son inherited the title Viscount Linley as a result.
(Wide World Photos)

In the Sixties, Margaret was much photographed: by her husband (above) and by Cecil Beaton (bottom photo).

(Wide World Photos)

By 1969, Margaret was looking less than blissful when snapped by Tony. *(Wide World Photos)*

These are the children that kept the marriage together for so long—Lady Sarah and Viscount Linley—with Mummy. *(Wide World Photos)*

The Snowdons tried to take an interest in the things one another held dear: in Tony's case, her horses; in Margaret's, his cameras. *(Wide World Photos)*

At public appearances, Tony had to settle for taking a back seat to his wife (above). But Margaret has had to accept the backseat herself whenever the Queen is present.

(top photo, Wide World Photos; bottom, Liaison Agency)

Before they'd been married seven years, Tony was being linked with other women—not always business associates like this blond executive.

(Liaison Agency)

Since her separation from her husband, Princess Margaret has been spending more time with her family, especially Viscount Linley and Sarah. *(Liaison Agency)*

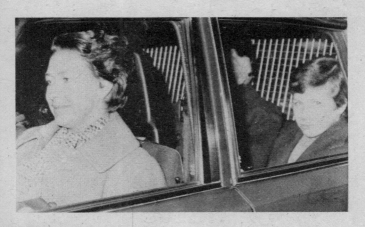

The marriage is over, but the lives go on. With her children, Margaret continues to attend many public functions while Tony pursues his thriving photography career and his fast-paced lifestyle.

(Wide World Photos)

Chapter Seven

The late forties and early fifties were an important time for Margaret, who had by that time totally ceased using her middle name, Rose, and relentlessly begun basking in her life as a popular young princess. This was the period of the "Margaret Set," when the princess became noted for being surrounded by a fast-moving crowd of peers and aristocrats, who were usually referred to simply as "Margaret's chinless wonders."

It was during this period that Margaret was first to learn the happiness of having babies underfoot, with Lilibet giving birth to her first two children, Charles and Anne. It was also the period of her deepest heartache, with the death of her beloved father closely followed by her thwarted relationship with Equerry of Honor Peter Townsend.

Margaret remained close to her sister Elizabeth after the princess and her new husband returned from their Birkhall honeymoon. When the two first got back to London, they stayed in a friend's "borrowed" house for a short period before moving into the refurbished Clarence House, an imposing structure into which Margaret and her mother would move following King George VI's death.

November 14, 1948 was a joyful day for the entire royal family. That was the day Elizabeth's first child, a son, was born. She and Philip had been happy to inform their relatives, not long after their wedding, that they were expecting their first addition. The king was especially pleased with the news of Lilibet's pregnancy, and he made no secret of his hopes that the baby would be a boy.

A grandson it was. Elizabeth and Philip demonstrated that they, too, had their iconoclastic streak by unpredictably naming the baby Charles III. This was a name no male of royal lineage had carried for three hundred years, since Charles II had been held in low esteem for so long. But the happy parents didn't worry about Charles II's many mistresses (who included Nell Gwynn and the Countess of Castlemaine) or his propensity for gambling. They considered that former monarch's kindness and generosity the features most worthy of note, and they proudly named their first son accordingly.

Margaret was ecstatic over the new arrival. When she hung up the telephone after receiving news of the baby's birth, she turned away with a glowing smile. "Hurray!" she announced. "I'm Charlie's aunt now." Leave it to the irrepressible Maggie to come up with a theatrical allusion for the blessed event.

On August 15, 1950, just a few days before Margaret's twentieth birthday, little Charles was joined by another baby. Elizabeth and Philip's second child was a girl, and they named her Anne.

With Lilibet married and busy with motherhood, Margaret was on her own more often now. The two sisters were still close and continued to spend a lot of time together. But Margaret was now spending more and more time with her parents, getting the kind of concentrated attention from the king and queen that she had always yearned for.

But, tragically, the king's health had already begun the steady decline that would lead to his early death.

The delicate physical health with which Bertie had struggled in his youth continued to plague him into adulthood. His gastritis was always with him and constantly flaring up. That was bad enough. But in 1948, the king began to have symptoms indicative of a serious new ailment as well.

The previous lack of stamina Bertie had exhibited had been put down to weariness and the aftermath of war. But World World II was now long over, and there was concern when the king began complaining of cramps in his legs and occasional pains in his chest. He was examined by four leading doctors who presented a joint diagnosis—the king had the beginnings of arteriosclerosis.

Arteriosclerosis consists of degenerative changes in the walls of the arteries. It is a condition that can be accompanied by several dreaded side effects. Arteries can become completely blocked, leading to thrombosis, gangrene, amputation. The pain that goes along with the disease is naggingly, excruciatingly constant.

And so it was that in February of 1949, Bertie underwent an operation to improve the flow of blood in his bad leg. It was a necessary step at that time, since it was feared the king was dangerously close to developing gangrene and losing his leg as a result of his condition.

Even in this strained, sad situation, the family showed their mettle. While still recovering from surgery, King George VI stylishly knighted the surgeon who had operated.

James Learmonth had called upon the king in his chambers for a final medical examination. After the exam had been concluded, the king, garbed in pajamas and a dressing gown, announced, "You used a knife on me, so now I am going to use one on you."

He then drew a sword from a nearby recess, asked the surgeon to kneel before him, and proclaimed him *Sir* James Learmonth. It just went to show how much poise and grace Bertie had developed over the years and how well he held onto it, even in sickness.

Also rising admirably to the situation of her father's ill health was young Princess Margaret. During the period of her father's recovery from surgery, she devoted herself entirely to him. There wasn't enough she could do for him, as far as she was concerned. She put herself completely at his disposal.

Almost every afternoon found Margaret in her father's room, chatting and reading to him, or off down the hall, playing the piano so that its strains would waft through his open bedroom door. As soon as he was strong enough to walk, it was Margaret who would escort him, gently mocking her diminutive size. "It's a blessing I'm not very tall," the five-feet one-inch tall princess told her father. "I make a good walking stick."

After the operation, the king was no longer bothered by his arteriosclerosis. His health seemed to be improving and under control, and those near to him heaved a collective sigh of relief. But it wasn't long before they realized their hopes for his good health were in vain. In a short time, he was suffering once again. But this time he was battling a far graver affliction. This time, it was cancer.

The difficulties the king had been having with

his chest and his breathing had at first been laid to bronchitis. But as the situation worsened, more tests were done, and by September, 1951, the doctors realized the king had cancer.

This time it was the queen, the strong-willed and capable Elizabeth Bowes-Lyon, who showed her strength. She was determined from the start that her husband should never learn the truth about his condition. She told those who knew to keep it from him. And as far as anyone knows, the king never suspected he was a victim of cancer, not even at the end.

It was in September that Bertie's doctors decided it was necessary to remove his left lung. The operation was performed September 23rd, just a month after Margaret's twenty-first birthday.

The king didn't suspect the real reason for the surgery. He was told he'd developed bronchial complications which necessitated removal of his lung. He did not question this explanation.

After surgery, the king appeared to rally. He seemed to be making a rapid recovery and was up and about quickly, almost his old self again. It was this upsurge that led King George VI's family to believe that he would fully recover, that the spread of the disease had been halted. But by the end of the year, Bertie was once again frail and ailing. By the time he gave his Christmas speech, his weak and weary voice testified to the seriousness of his ill health.

On January 31, 1952, Princess Elizabeth and

Prince Philip departed on the first stage of a tour to East Africa, Australia and New Zealand. The tour had originally been planned for the king and queen. But now the king was too weak to risk such strenuous travel. It was decided to send his daughter in his place.

And so, just six days before he was to lose his battle with death, King George VI stood on the runway at London Airport, watching the departure of his daughter and her husband. His wife stood protectively on one side of him; Margaret stood on the other. Bareheaded in the chilly air, bundled into a heavy coat, Bertie appeared haggard and drawn. He was obviously not a well man. As Elizabeth's plane took off, he followed it with his eyes and murmured, "I don't know how we'll manage for five months without Lilibet."

On February 5th, the family was ensconced at Sandringham, leading a quiet life so the king could get as much rest as possible. That particular day had been a good one. Bertie had gone out shooting in the afternoon, bagging some hares and a pigeon. After dinner, he listened to the radio with his wife and Margaret, to the broadcast of the reception given Elizabeth and Philip in Kenya.

When the king decided to retire early, the queen gave orders that he was not to be disturbed after he drank his bedtime cup of cocoa. He would sleep, as usual, with his door open, so the servants could hear him if he needed anything during the night.

The king didn't call out, and when his valet, James MacDonald, brought morning tea at 7:30 the following day, he expected to find everything as usual. But when he entered the king's bedroom, he found the king seeming to be still asleep. Then, when MacDonald attempted to rouse the king, he discovered the truth. King George VI was dead. He had died in his sleep.

MacDonald went immediately to inform the king's widow, who accepted the sad news with the composure and grace common to her. Upon hearing that her husband was dead, she was silent a moment, then quietly said, "We must tell Elizabeth. We must tell—the queen."

The report of her father's death had to be relayed to Elizabeth in Kenya. When Elizabeth and Philip stepped off their plane from Africa, the new queen was already dressed in black for her father's funeral.

On February 15, 1952, King George VI was buried at Windsor. Little more than a month later, on March 24th of that same year, his mother followed him to the grave. The death of Queen Mary so soon after their beloved Bertie's plunged the royal family even deeper into grief. And a nation—the empire which was to shrink into a loose group of Commonwealth countries during the reign of Elizabeth II—mourned.

Margaret was devastated by her father's death. She was just twenty-one, a young enough age to lose a parent. And now she was losing her sister, too, watching Elizabeth thrust more than ever into a different realm. Now Lilibet was queen. Margaret belonged less than ever.

But, with her usual spirit, Margaret wouldn't be crushed by her own heartache. When Elizabeth returned to Sandringham, on the third day following her father's death, Margaret was there to greet her. She presented herself to Lilibet with a curtsy for the first time—a curtsy to her sister's new role as Queen Elizabeth II.

Sadly, it seemed as if it had been only a year or two before that she and Lilibet had greeted their wonderful Papa with a historic curtsy. It was 1936, when he had returned home from his meeting at St. James, no longer the duke of York but suddenly the king of England.

The former queen, Margaret and Lilibet's mother, decided to take the title of Queen Mother, so that she wouldn't create a confusion of names for her daughter, now Elizabeth II. Grief-stricken though she was, the king's widow never lost her poise. Nor did she for a moment forget her duty to the British crown, to the royal position she had once dreaded.

The Queen Mother had by now committed herself to a life of dedication to duty and responsibility, the life prophesied for her at her wedding ceremony by the archbishop of York. And so, as she thanked the people of Great Britain for their sympathy and kindness during her time of mourning, she told them, "Throughout our married life, we have tried, the king and I, to fulfill with all our hearts and all our strength the great task of service that was laid upon us. My only wish is now that I may be allowed to continue the work we sought to do together."

There was nothing people wanted more than to keep the Queen Mother as part of their lives. To this day, the Queen Mother has remained active, beloved and omnipresent, a true symbol of British refinement.

It was to her mother that Margaret's thoughts immediately turned following the king's death. She stayed by her mother's side, and though the physician at Sandringham prescribed sedatives for her, Margaret refused to take them. She wanted to be alert in case her mother needed her.

This was an exceptionally painful period for Margaret. Her thoughts, her cares, were mostly for others. For her mother, bereaved and alone. For her sister, who now had the weight of the throne on her shoulders. For herself, Margaret gave little consideration. Several months after George VI's death, she was still refusing invitations so she could keep an eye on his widow. "I can't go away this weekend," she told one friend who had invited her to the country. "I mustn't leave Mummy alone."

Margaret's grief led her to turn to religion, something she would do again later, when she would find it difficult to cope with her inner turmoil over the Peter Townsend affair. Now, in 1952, she attended a series of eleven half-hour lectures at St. Paul's in Knightsbridge.

The religious lectures made an impression on

Margaret, and she would often discuss them afterwards with Dr. Fisher, the archbishop of Canterbury, in his chambers at Lambeth Palace.

Later Dr. Fisher remembered, "Every meeting with her was a sort of friendly argument. She was always friendly, always intelligent, but would state her views and would let me state my views, which we would discuss and argue, talking things over in this free and open way.... I came to be especially devoted to her. I knew what a genuine concern she had in the life of the Church and the life of a churchwoman."

It was within her religion that Margaret sought solace during this trying time, a period that climaxed with Elizabeth and Philip moving into Buckingham Palace and Margaret and the Queen Mother moving out. In point of fact, they switched residences, since Margaret and her mother moved into Clarence House.

On June 2, 1953, the world watched on television as one of the most historic days in British history unfolded. Queen Elizabeth II's coronation was a stirring event. It had everything the romance-nurtured world of the fifties could hope for—a lovely young queen, her handsome prince consort, her pretty little sister, her regal mother. And, of course, there was all the legendary pomp and circumstance which had accompanied George VI's coronation more than fifteen years before.

One of the highlights of the coronation was Philip's speech. Hearts around the world were set aflutter when the consort knelt before his wife, the queen, in Westminster Abbey and vowed, "I, Philip, Duke of Edinburgh, do become your liege man of life and limb and earthly worship, and faith and truth will I bear unto you, to live and die against all manner of folks. So help me God."

Those were words to set Margaret's heart racing. She was a born fantasist, an incurable romantic, an impressionable young woman. She was also party to a romance that would soon put the capper on the wild reputation she had been getting in recent years. The "Margaret Set" was racy enough. But Margaret's romance with Peter Townsend was going to be much more newsworthy and stunning. It would divide people all over the globe into two distinct camps—those rallying to the side of Margaret and true love, and those siding with the Church of England and propriety. And, as she watched her sister being crowned as queen of England, as she listened to Philip's avowal of love, Margaret must have been powerfully moved by the passionate aspect of it all. She herself was in love with Peter Townsend and had already told Lilibet that nothing would make her happier than to become his wife.

Chapter Eight

As she entered into her early twenties, Princess Margaret was considered one of the most eligible women in the world. She was a very personable young lady, and certainly a most attractive one, carrying a scant one hundred pounds nicely distributed on her petite frame. A magazine article of the times revealed her body measurements to be: bust, 33½; waist, 21½; hips, 33. Time had not yet taken its toll on the princess's hourglass figure.

Margaret was considered a very pretty and presentable young princess, but she was also rated a trifle wild. After her father's death, public criticism regarding the young princess was rampant. Though she had led an unbelievably quiet life immediately following his death, devoting her time to her mother and her thoughts to religion, she drifted into a different mode of existence after the pain of her bereavement had lessened. Then, as if in defiance of mortality, she let her hair down and began living it up in earnest.

Fault-finding with Margaret ranged from pointing out the fact that her makeup was too "tarty" and her clothes too daring to advancing the theory that it was unwholesome for youthful royalty to hobnob with such American "music hall" entertainers as Danny Kaye.

Margaret's public smoking was also frowned upon. Although she puffed her French Gitane cigarettes daintily, with the aid of a long cigarette-holder, smoking by "nice" young women was simply not done in those unliberated days of the 1950s.

If that weren't bad enough, Margaret was spotted too often and too late in West End clubs where the customers were judged unsavory. And when she and her close friend Sharman Douglas, the United States ambassador's daughter, danced a mild cancan at a charity ball, myriad eyes rolled in displeasure. As far as most proper Britons were concerned, this wasn't the way a royal princess was supposed to behave.

How did Margaret become so bohemian? One could blame her desire for freedom for propelling her into a life of burning the candle at both ends. Now that she was old enough to sample and savor life as she liked, Margaret didn't wish to miss a minute of it. She had missed out again and again in her childhood. Now that she was a grownup, she wanted to experience *everything*.

At eighteen, Margaret was allowed her first lady-in-waiting. She chose Jennifer Bevan, who is now Mrs. John Lowther and still a close friend. Miss Bevan was just four years Margaret's senior, twenty-two at the time.

As Margaret's lady-in-waiting, Miss Bevan was called upon to accompany the princess to places royalty had never even *considered* visiting. For instance, when she was still a teenager, Margaret decided that she wanted to see a newspaper put to bed. So late one night off she went to the *Daily Graphic* offices in Fleet Street with her lady-in-waiting by her side.

Margaret didn't want to read about things or hear about things. She'd had enough of *that* in her childhood. Now, she wanted to *do* things, to see them happen. So, another time, she took Miss Bevan off to the Central Criminal Courts at the Old Bailey so she could watch a murder trial in progress. And, on yet another excursion, she dropped in at Scotland Yard for a visit, where she asked to be fingerprinted. Needless to say, the amused constables were quick to oblige. They duly inked her fingers and presented her with a set of prints.

Though Margaret had her own Rolls-Royce, with a license registration mark that proclaimed "P.M.," she wasn't encouraged to drive it herself. She would usually sit in the back seat with her lady-in-waiting. Up front, her chauffeur would drive, a plainclothes detective from Scotland Yard by his side.

So Margaret entered adulthood the same way she had passed through childhood—on the one hand, precocious and headstrong; on the other, protected and sheltered. As children, she and Lilibet had been allowed to visit the same spots where other British children went sightseeing—the Regents Park Zoo, the London and British Museums, the Royal Tournament, Victoria and Albert Museum. But Margaret and Lilibet had seen those places through different eyes from the rest of the kiddies; Margaret and Lilibet had always been the two Little Princesses, accompanied by their retinue of governesses and nannies.

Now, life for Margaret was in many ways the same. She went out a great deal more often than she had as a child, and she visited more public places. But her excursions were still supervised and regulated. She was still the imprisoned princess pretending to be free.

Margaret never carried money, for instance, except on those rare occasions when she went someplace without her lady-in-waiting. As a matter of fact, nary a mention of anything as common as filthy lucre had to fall from Margaret's lips. Her lady-in-waiting handled everything. This meant that whenever Margaret went shopping, her lady-in-waiting would accompany her from store to store, staying in the background as Margaret browsed, discreetly informing each shop manager to send a bill to Buckingham

Palace for whatever items the princess chose. At a party or a dance, Margaret never parceled out tips to the ladies' room attendants. The lady-in-waiting would hand the attendant Margaret's gratuity, a half crown, which in its United States equivalent of thirty-five cents was double the usual tip. In nightclubs or restaurants, somewhat of the same procedure would take place. Margaret's lady-in-waiting would telephone to make the reservation and inform the manager at that time to send a bill to the palace. Margaret was never directly presented with a check.

So there she was, spoiled and pampered, never having to fend for herself, yet still made an outcast by the very rank that made her life so luxurious. As she grew up, Margaret grew more like everyone else, but that wasn't the same as being like everyone else. It's no wonder she grew up confused, given to attacks of migraine and fits of depression. Margaret was never certain whether she should be playing the princess or the plebe.

Just consider the type of upbringing in which everything is laid at one's feet, and how little that upbringing prepares one to deal with real life. For example, when Margaret, at the age of fifteen, had appendicitis, it wasn't even considered for a moment that she might do what other people did and enter a hospital. No, the hospital came to her instead, in the persons of the doctors and nurses of the Great Ormond Street Hospital. The operation was performed in Margaret's own pale pink bedroom at Buckingham Palace, and during her convalescence, she was surrounded not by a group of impersonal strangers, but by her own family and their staff. Pampering certainly had its good points.

But pampering had its drawbacks as well. A sheltered life, Margaret learned, was as much of a prison as it was a palace. By the time she was in her twenties, Margaret had never even been on a real date, just herself and one man. Instead, she always had to go out in groups, or with several men. She had *never* been out in public all by herself, only with a governess or a nanny or a lady-in-waiting or a detective. Solitary walks through foggy London streets were not hers for the asking.

Nor had Princess Margaret even been to a school. She had been educated solely through private lessons. She knew little about the activities of what the rest of the world considered everyday life. Margaret was a princess, but she was also, in a manner of speaking, a pariah.

It was Margaret's refusal to bow down to her role, her adamant defiance of staid standards, that led her to cause raised eyebrows wherever she went. At fourteen, she was caught red-handed in the act of sampling her father's champagne—she was already eager to see what life would have to offer her when she grew up.

As she grew older, Margaret continued to delight in embellishing her own iconoclastic behavior. She once elicited stunned laughter when she bade farewell to the Governor of Kenya with the then-popular catch-phrase, "See you later, alligator." She wanted very much to be unique, to be a personality, to be not just another dull princess. But, at the same time, Margaret wanted all the prerogatives of her position. She had no interest in giving up any of the "perks" that went with being a member of royalty. She wanted all the respect she felt she deserved. She didn't mind that even her closest friends called her "Ma'am." In short, she wanted the world.

By 1949, Britain's social diarist Mr. "Chips" Channon was already remarking that the young Princess Margaret had "a Marie Antoinette aroma" about her. Yes, she was well on her way to becoming a history-making woman. By the 1950s, she was cultivating her "aroma" in earnest.

Margaret was never averse to being in the public eye. It was deciding the manner in which she wanted to present herself that was a problem. She was never quite sure which public image would be best for which occasion. But she was happy to have a distinct image in any event. Once, when she was asked if she hadn't found it embarrassing to be stared at so much during her life, Margaret answered, "It's strange, but somehow, right from the beginning, I don't seem to remember noticing."

Another part of what being a princess was all about consisted of having a mad whirl of a social life. Margaret had many beaux before unwisely falling for that least eligible man of them all, Peter Townsend. At seventeen, she had been linked with Prince Michael of Rumania. At eighteen, it was Lord Blandford who was squiring her around. At nineteen, there was a different lord in Margaret's life, Lord Ogilvy. But the next year, Ogilvy had been replaced, and Margaret's new favorite escort was Lord Dalkeith. And there were still others. Margaret was linked with Billy Wallace, Mark Bonham Carter, Lord Hambleton, Collin Tennant, gentleman farmer Robin McEwen, Lord "Jimmy" Carnegie, Lord Plunket, Lord Porchester and the Honorable Peter Ward. Princess Margaret was certainly never lacking for dates.

She was rather blasé about the whole social whirlwind. She did enjoy it, and her ego was nurtured—as any young woman's would be—by the attention and the publicity. But Margaret couldn't really take any of it seriously. She saw the silliness of the social swing.

Once, when she was a mere eighteen, Margaret was dancing at a ball when she suddenly ordered her startled dancing partner, "Look into my eyes."

"I am looking into them, Ma'am," the young man quickly replied.

"Well," Margaret informed him archly, "you're looking into the most beautiful eyes in England. The duchess of Kent has the most beautiful nose. The duchess of Windsor has the most beautiful chin. And I have the most beautiful eyes."

As the young man continued to look puzzled, Margaret smiled teasingly, "Surely, you believe what you read in the papers." Yes, the precocious child had grown into a most precocious young woman.

By eighteen, Margaret was already a budding femme fatale. She had been practicing for years. As young as sixteen, she'd developed a tendency to douse herself with Schiaparelli's "shocking" scent. That was the age, too, when she had insisted upon wearing lipstick, much to the chagrin of her conservative mother.

When Margaret had first brought up the subject of lipstick, the queen had tried to veto the suggestion. "Do you really think it's becoming?" she had asked delicately, hoping Margaret would agree it was not. But the girl's mother was to have no such luck. Margaret answered by dragging the queen to see a movie short that featured the royal family, in which Elizabeth had worn lipstick while Margaret and the queen wore none.

"See, Mummy," Margaret said contemptuously, "you and I look like suet dumplings!"

Lipstick wasn't the only aspect of style Margaret followed. She was always eager to be in the swing of things, and, as a result, she and her mother often disagreed when it came to choosing her clothes. Margaret was fast gaining a reputation as a daring dresser. She wanted to be free to pick and choose her own clothes from among the lines of the more fashionable young designers rather than be resigned to a life of tweeds, tartans and Norman Hartnell dresses.

"I do not desire to be a leader of fashion," the

queen told her, in an attempt to justify her taste in clothing.

"Well," replied daughter Margaret, sticking resolutely to her guns, "I do."

Today, Margaret's interest in fashion has inclined, in the family manner, towards dowdiness. But she's still noted for her inability to decide whether she wants to be treated like just plain folk or like Her Royal Highness Princess Margaret. This ambiguity steadily developed throughout the fifties. Margaret liked being treated as a special being, adored being kowtowed to, but wasn't always satisfied with her life. Sometimes being different wasn't all that terrific. That's what propelled the princess to turn to her father, in the midst of the royal family's tour to South Africa in 1947, and murmur, "Isn't it a pity that we have to travel with royalty?"

Margaret missed being able to savor the average life. Still, she wouldn't have traded places with a commoner for anything. She was just betwixt and between.

All in all, Margaret had no choice in the matter, anyhow. She was royalty, and that was all there was to it. She had been born to a position of privilege. There was nothing she could do to change the station of her birth and all the amenities that went with it. Nor could she wiggle out of the chores, duties and drawbacks of that position.

The state of being what Britons term "a royal" was best summed up by Margaret's paternal grandmother, Queen Mary. The dowager queen was once listening to a relative complain about having to visit so many hospitals. Queen Mary had no truck with complainers, and she reminded this one, "You are a member of the British royal family. We are *never* tired and we all *love* hospitals."

At seventeen, Margaret was already being called upon to do some of these things, and she was already showing her talent at handling royal duties. She proved to those who had worried about her poise that, when she wanted to be perfect, few could top her.

The specific occasion was the launching of a liner in Northern Ireland. Margaret, representing the monarchy, was presented with a bouquet of roses by a shy fifteen-year-old joiner's apprentice named Tommy Smith. As she took the flowers, Margaret appeared to be fumbling with them. No one could fathom what she was doing. But at last she removed a single rose from the bunch and slipped it into the happily blushing young man's buttonhole. Margaret had made a special occasion even more memorable, and the crowd cheered her lovingly. Such was her charm, even while only an adolescent, when she chose to turn it on.

This was the young Princess Margaret who fell under the spell of the handsome airman Peter Townsend. She was no demure babe in arms. She was a capable young woman very much in possession of a mind of her own. She was lovely, a petite young thing with style and verve, but she was never weak or easily led.

And she could have had her choice of men. Margaret was escorted by the pick of the crop of the globe's eligible bachelors. She was wined and dined by the handsomest, most socially connected men in England, and she was not naive when it came to feminine wiles. She loved to flirt and play the vamp. She was a young woman who could have had anything she wanted.

And then one day she announced that the one thing she wanted was the thing she could *not* have—a middle-aged divorced man, a commoner whose first marriage had ended badly. Princess Margaret didn't want the world—she wanted only Peter Townsend.

Chapter Nine

Today, recalling Margaret's romance with Peter Townsend has little shock value. It wasn't as if he were a married man. His marriage was already ended by the time the young princess realized her feeling for him. And, though a commoner, Peter wasn't exactly riffraff. If the Townsend affair were to happen today, it's doubtful that there would be any turmoil at all. Margaret probably would have married him, and that would have been that. But, in considering the way royalty behaves, 1955 seems more like two centuries ago than just two short decades.

The love story of the princess and the pilot spans several years. By 1953, Princess Margaret knew she was in love with Townsend. She knew Peter was the one man who could make her happy.

Margaret had always been fond of Peter. She had liked him for his gentle spirit, admired him for his quiet intelligence. When her father died, Margaret learned that Peter was also a man of strength, a man upon whom she could lean.

It was after the death of George VI that the friendship between his daughter Margaret and Peter Townsend, the man he would have liked as a son, grew more serious. It deepened steadily, bit by bit, until one day both of them realized the truth. There was no denying their love for each other.

There was an age difference—Townsend was in his late thirties, Margaret was in her twenties—but that wasn't so shocking. What was all the commotion about, then? The simple fact that Peter Townsend was a divorced man was more than enough to upset this romantic apple cart. The Church of England, with Queen Elizabeth II as its head, was opposed categorically to divorce. In the eyes of the Church of England, Margaret could not marry a man who had been wed before.

Back in 1939, when she was still Princess Elizabeth, the queen had addressed two thousand people at a Mothers' Union Rally in London and told them her feelings about marriage. "When we see around us the havoc which has been wrought, above all among the children," she intoned, "by the break-up of homes, we can have no doubt that divorce and separation are responsible for some of the darkest evil in our society today." Divorce was taboo, regardless of the problems involved.

In Townsend's case, the break-up certainly hadn't been his doing. He was considered the innocent party when, six days before Christmas in 1952, he was granted a decree nisi of divorce on grounds of his wife's misconduct at a London hotel in August, 1951. An order of custody of their two sons was granted to Peter, but, by consent, the care and control of the children was to remain with their mother until further order of the court.

The consensus at the time was that Peter and his wife had been pulled apart by the demands of his career. His work always was first with him, and, especially after he joined the royal household, Peter was away more and more, devoting himself to the needs and wishes of his king. He traveled often, leaving his wife alone with their children in the little grace-and-favor cottage. Out of loneliness, she turned elsewhere for solace and companionship. The result was that a marriage ended. Like so many endings, it was more sad than ugly.

After the divorce, the former Mrs. Townsend married John de Lazlo, the corespondent in the divorce suit, while Peter explained away his marriage to friends by saying, "We had only known each other for six weeks. Ridiculous, wasn't it?" Whatever it was, the marriage was over. And in the meantime, the relationship with Margaret was begun and just about to explode into headlines.

It was at the coronation of Queen Elizabeth II

that a sharp-eyed reporter in a Westminster Abbey anteroom happened to spy Princess Margaret affectionately brushing off the lapels of airman Townsend's jacket. The gesture was one of possessive "wifeliness"—similar to the one which had set off the brouhaha regarding Margaret's Uncle David and his romance with Wallis Simpson. That time, it had been a watchful photographer who had caught the lady with her hand on the king's wrist.

Of course, Margaret's relationship with Townsend wasn't exactly the same kettle of fish as David's romance had been. As Edward VIII, David had been the king-emperor, the personal embodiment of the sovereign power in a Britain which was still governed by prim Victorian standards. Margaret, on the other hand, was a princess living in a predominantly socialist-minded state. She had little chance of ascending to the throne. Thus, her relationship with Peter gave little reason to create such a crisis amongst the rest of the royal family and so much alarm within the British government and the Church of England. But it did. It created them in abundance.

It was an age-old love story—duty on one side versus desire on the other. Margaret was in love with the dashing pilot, the tall, slender, handsome war hero.. And he loved her in return. Once the press got wind of their romance, there was no stopping the stories. Love was always news. Love between a princess and a divorced commoner— that was *big* news. Photographers all over

England kept a sharp lookout for Townsend's little green Renault, hoping to get more shots of the princess and the pilot *à deux*. And stories of one sort or another about the duo abounded.

Finally, in 1955, even the conservative British humor magazine *Punch* got into the act by printing a cartoon which showed an impressionable little girl counting the peas on her dinner plate to the words, "Tinker, tailor, soldier .... group captain." The romance was in the news so often that rarely a day went by without an item on Margaret and Peter. One BBC comedian cashed in on this to get a big laugh. He asked his straight man to read the news of the day. "They had tea together again," the other intoned resignedly, to much laughter. Everyone had something to say about Peter and Margaret, and everyone wanted to know what they were up to and to chart the course of their love.

The course was not running smoothly. The pressure on Margaret at the time was close to unbearable. At one emotional session during *l'affaire* Townsend, Margaret reportedly told her sister, her beloved Lilibet, "You look after your empire and leave me alone." But she knew even at the time that this was impossible.

Put simply, the queen had to do everything in her power to dissuade Margaret from marrying Townsend. Or at least that was the way she saw it. There were several powerful persons opposed to the idea of Margaret's marrying the flyer, and they were all pressuring Queen Elizabeth to use every ounce of her influence on her younger sister. These included Robert Cecil, the marquess of Salisbury, who was Anthony Eden's chief representative in the House of Lords and very influential in government; Geoffrey Francis Fisher, the archbishop of Canterbury and, next to the queen herself, the highest official in the Anglican Church, besides being a very close friend of the princess; and Prince Philip, the queen's own husband, who had never particularly cared for Townsend and who felt that Margaret had no business even considering marriage to the man. The queen, who so loved her younger sister, was having a difficult time of it herself, being torn in her feelings and besieged with opinions and pressure from every side.

Lilibet would have loved to have seen her sister happy—as long as it meant anything else besides marriage to Peter Townsend. George VI had educated his elder daughter to be a monarch; the result was that Britain and its policies were the focal points of the queen's life, not personal happiness. In Elizabeth II's opinion, as in her mother's and father's before her, doing one's duty to the crown was what counted most.

In 1951, the queen gave a speech at the unveiling in the Mall of a memorial statue of George VI. She told the crowd assembled for the event, "Much was asked of my father in personal sacrifice and endeavor. He shirked no task, however difficult, and to the end, he never faltered in his duty." Lilibet wished only to live as her father had done, by his set of rules, and she fervently hoped that Margaret would decide to do the same.

Not everyone agreed with the queen. When the London *Daily Mirror* ran a public opinion poll, the results showed that the mass of the people were on Margaret's side. The paper stated the situation between the twenty-two-year-old princess and the thirty-eight-year-old pilot, then asked that all-important question. Should Margaret be allowed to marry the man?

Votes poured in from all over the country, and the result was that an astounding 96.81 percent were in favor of the marriage, with a mere 3.19 percent opposed to the union. Margaret's own sister was indeed in the minority.

But what a powerful minority that was. It was the minority into which Princess Margaret had been born, and even she understood the responsibility she was supposed to have to the concept of duty.

In Wiltshire to present a new set of colors to the First Battalion of the Highland Light Infantry, Margaret pushed aside her own unhappiness to tell the soldiers, "History is not made by a few outstanding actions. It is made remorselessly . . . by devotion to duty, by steadiness in times of anxiety, by discipline in waiting." It was as if she were speaking to herself as well, giving herself a private lecture on obligation and self-sacrifice. But could she actually do what her Uncle David hadn't been capable of doing? Could Margaret give up a great love for the call of duty?

It was difficult to predict, and the waiting period, while Margaret made up her mind whether to continue her relationship with Townsend or break it off, was not without irony. At one point, Margaret helped the queen entertain the visiting president of Portugal, which included sitting through a performance of Smetana's *The Battered Bride*, an opera which included a soprano singing to a forbidden lover, "Nothing in the world will ever part us." The situation was ironic—and very painful.

In 1955, *Time* magazine's London Bureau chief Andre Laguerre cabled New York and summed up the entire furor over the Peter Townsend problem this way:

"Britons today lack much of their old self-confidence," he stated. "The recent advent of a young queen, the talk of a new Elizabethan era, the dynamic character of a new self-confident Toryism, the conquest of Everest by Edmund Hillary and of time by four-minute miler Roger Bannister, are all factors which in the last few years have combined to bolster that waning confidence. Princess Margaret will start no revolution whatever she may do, but things are now so far advanced that if, in the end, she gives up Townsend, the outcome will be highly unpopular with many Britons, an unpopularity essentially derived not from the feeling that stuffiness had conquered love, but from the conviction that her choice was not a free one.

"By slackly refusing to recognize the crisis until it was on them, by allowing its final moments to be played out in the heat of controversy and the glare of publicity, the royal family and the Eden government have put themselves in a position where they cannot win. If, at the last minute, they persuade Margaret to send Townsend away, they will be undemocratic bullies in the eyes of many. If they give even reluctant consent, they will offend many others."

The furor over the Townsend business grew by the day, until finally it seemed as if everyone in England was wondering if Margaret and Peter would marry. Finally, the palace issued its first statement on the subject. An official announcement was sent out, stating, "In view of the varied reports which have been published, the Press Secretary to the queen is authorized to say that no announcement concerning Princess Margaret's personal future is at present contemplated. The Princess Margaret has asked the Press Secretary to express the hope that the press and public will extend to Her Royal Highness their customary courtesy and cooperation in respecting her privacy."

In other words, no one had very much to say on the subject, neither Margaret herself nor the queen.

On the princess's twenty-fifth birthday, in August of 1955, she was in Balmoral with the Queen Mother. When her mother asked her if she was still determined to marry Peter, Margaret said yes. The Queen Mother still didn't approve. But she did want her daughter to find happiness. Like her daughter the queen, she was torn between love and obligation when it came to her daughter the princess. She told Margaret a marriage would be possible only under three conditions.

The first condition was that Margaret and Townsend would wed not in a church but in a registry office. The second was that Margaret would renounce all claims to the throne and to the fifteen thousand pounds due her on her wedding. And the third was that she and her husband, Peter, should agree to live in exile for a while.

Were all these drastic conditions necessary? The answer would appear to be an emphatic no. For instance, there was absolutely no reason why Margaret should have felt compelled to live in exile after making a marriage of which approximately ninety eight percent of all Britons approved. And, even if she had agreed to give up her royal dowry, Margaret wouldn't have had to settle for a life of abject poverty. Queen Elizabeth II is one of the world's richest women. She could easily have settled a million or two pounds on her sister from the large estate that had been left by Queen Mary. In short, Margaret was being told she could go ahead and marry Townsend, while still being not too subtly pressured to give him up.

Townsend, in the meantime, was no longer in the country. He was residing in Brussels, having been "transferred" out of England, the better to give Margaret some distance and room to think.

In October of 1955, Peter arrived back in London, on vacation from Brussels, and he visited Clarence House. When he left that building, after having taken tea with Margaret and her mother, reporters were waiting outside to ask, "Are you happy?"

When Peter answered, "Yes," everyone imagined that the best had happened—that he and Margaret were indeed being granted permission to wed.

But that wasn't so. Shortly afterwards, Peter ended up cutting short, by three days, his leave in England. He left London to resume his exile as an air attaché in Brussels after telling reporters, "I am not unhappy, you know, not unhappy at all." But he added, "Of course I shall never be able to speak to you freely."

Up until this point, everyone had imagined that the wheels were being set in motion for Margaret to marry Townsend. Now no one was sure what was going on. And everyone suspected the worst.

On her birthday, Margaret had attended services in the Crathie Church in Balmoral, where the Reverend John Lamb had prayed, "Grant unto her now of Thy Grace, the fullness of Thy blessing is that, trusting in Thee, she may find fulfillment of her heart's desires, that joy may be her heritage and peace her portion."

Alas, Margaret was not to find fulfillment of her heart's desires. Instead, she was to choose to give it all up in the name of obligation to her royal duties.

The archbishop later said that Randolph

Churchill was incorrect and that he had never been seated in his study when Margaret entered to tell him, "Archbishop, you may put your books away: I have made up my mind."

In recalling his meeting with the princess on the last weekend in October, 1955, Dr. Fisher remembered, "The princess came and I received her in the quiet of my own study. But she never said, 'Put away those books.' There were not any books to put away. Her decision was purely on the grounds of conscience. When it became clear what God's will was, she did it, and that is not a bad thing for people in general to note."

What Margaret did was to issue a statement directly from Clarence House on the evening of October 31st. "I would like it to be known," she said, "that I have decided not to marry Group Captain Peter Townsend. I have been aware that, subject to my renouncing my rights of succession, it might have been possible for me to contract a civil marriage. But, mindful of the Church's teaching that Christian marriage is indissoluble, and conscious of my duty to the Commonwealth, I have resolved to put these considerations before any others.

"I have reached this decision entirely alone," her statement went on, "and in doing so I have been strengthened by the unfailing support and devotion of Group Captain Townsend. I am deeply grateful for the concern of all those who have constantly prayed for my happiness." The statement was signed simply "Margaret."

132

Giving up the man she loved was a great sacrifice to make. Certainly, it was an enormous one for the young woman who had always felt that she deserved freedom and happiness and who always worried that neither was within her grasp. Margaret's love for Townsend was deep and genuine. She even kept photographs of the group captain on her bedroom table for several years after they parted. But for once in her life, perhaps for the last time, Margaret allowed her sense of obligation to win out. She gave up Peter Townsend—who eventually married another.

Later, the archbishop of Canterbury, interviewed on the BBC regarding Princess Margaret's decision, said, "Of course she took advice. She got plenty of advice, asked for, and a good deal more unasked for. In the end, it was her own decision, and she was under no pressure from state or Church."

The fact that Margaret denied having been pressured by the Church did nothing to halt rumors early in 1956 to the effect that she was giving up the Anglican religion and converting to Catholicism. These rumors took three forms: the first was that Margaret just wanted to be a Catholic rather than a member of the Church of England; the second insisted that she was hoping that if she and Peter Townsend both converted, they could wed; and the third was to the effect that Margaret was converting in order to marry Belgium's Catholic King Baudouin.

These rumors, all totally false, were fired by a

trip to Rome by the Roman Catholic duke of Norfolk. The duke, a Premier Peer and hereditary Earl Marshal of England, went to call on the pope for the first time in eighteen years. But his visit turned out to have nothing to do with Margaret, as a harassed official of London's Roman Catholic Westminster Cathedral had to explain again and again.

"I have been denying these rumors fourteen times daily for the last four days," the man said in dismay. "No prayers for the conversion of Princess Margaret have been offered."

He was correct. There were no prayers for her conversion, and Princess Margaret remained an unmarried member of the Anglican Church. But there were many prayers said for her all over the world. People prayed for the proud young woman so unlucky in love, for the princess trapped in her ivory tower. They hoped she would be able to find happiness and love.

But in the period immediately following the end of her relationship with Peter Townsend, Margaret was looking for neither happiness nor love. She was seeking forgetfulness, abandonment. The bitter taste of her doomed romance was still too strong to allow her to seek another. She had loved this one man too dearly, and, in losing him, she had lost the desire to play the game.

Was the Peter Townsend episode the most crucial in Margaret's life? Undoubtedly. If she had received support and encouragement from those nearest to her, she would most certainly have married the man. To say that she was not pressured into giving up Peter Townsend would be tantamount to insisting that King Edward VIII could have had Wallis Warfield Simpson and the throne as well.

If Princess Margaret had married Townsend, her life would have taken a far different course. But fate had other plans in store for her. Instead of marrying the tall, aloof pilot, Margaret would marry the short, gregarious photographer. Antony Armstrong-Jones was the man who would become Princess Margaret's husband, the man who would have to cope with the long-lasting aftermath of the world's famous story of thwarted royal love.

Chapter Ten

In 1952, an up-and-coming young photographer named Antony Armstrong-Jones was asked by a friend whom he would most like to photograph. Without a moment's hesitation, he answered, "Why, Princess Margaret, of course. I think she's the most vivacious person in the world."

The princess was not feeling particularly vivacious at the time, so perhaps it was just as well the two didn't meet then. Margaret's beloved father had just died, and her feelings for Peter Townsend were leading her into an upsetting situation. In general, she wasn't in her best frame of mind.

Margaret wouldn't make the acquaintance of the young photographer for several years. By the time she did meet Antony Armstrong-Jones, he seemed a far better choice for a husband than the departed Townsend could ever have been.

Tony Armstrong-Jones is a fascinating man from a notable background. The Armstrong-Jones family originated in Wales, where they used to be just plain Jones, and where they had as their motto the phrase "A Noddo Dow A Noddir," which translates as "To support God is to be supported." By the time he met Margaret, young Armstrong-Jones was supporting himself quite well as a photographer, and was a polished member of London's more "in" bohemian set.

His family background was very acceptable on paper, even though his parents had divorced shortly after his birth. Tony's father, Ronald Owen Lloyd Armstrong-Jones, had inherited a small fortune in the hundreds of thousands of dollars, from his father, Sir Robert, who was also responsible for adding the Armstrong to the family name in 1913.

Tony's father, a barrister, would later remarry, taking a much younger woman, a former B.O.A.C. air hostess, for his new wife. Tony's mother, the countess of Rosse, was the innocent party in the divorce action. Ironically, she later did exactly what Margaret and Peter Townsend hadn't been allowed to do—she remarried in a London church.

Tony was born March 7, 1930. He'd had some artistic blood coursing through his veins from the start; his mother's brother, Oliver Messel, was a renowned set designer. But Tony grew interested in the arts only after he contracted a childhood case of polio.

Before being stricken, Tony was mostly interested in boxing, and he had won several interschool bouts for Eton when he was in attendance there. Before that, he'd matriculated at the Sandroyd School. It was while at Eton that he came down with the illness which would leave him with a slight limp. And it was during his convalescence that Tony's mother presented him with his first camera.

After his recovery, Tony went back to his studies, but he no longer took them with any degree of seriousness. Perhaps his bout with illness had given him a different slant on life and reformed his ideas about what was important and what wasn't. In any event, he did not exactly shine when he was at Jesus College at Cambridge as an architectural student. After two years he was "sent down"—which is to say, expelled—for what he later ambiguously termed the "usual high jinks."

While at Cambridge, Tony had taken pictures of various sporting events for their newspaper, the *Varsity*. The paper didn't like his photographs well enough to keep him on the staff, but, as news-happy journalists do, they were grateful enough for the chance to use him a few years later in a terse banner headline on his engagement: PRINCESS TO MARRY MAN WE FIRED.

As a youth, Tony was always extremely sensitive about the leg weakness he retained as a result of his polio attack. His limp was barely noticeable; one leg was a tiny bit thinner than the other. Still, he would rarely wear shorts or a bathing suit, and he seldom danced. His bad leg also made him exempt from military service.

In more recent times, the British satirical magazine, *Private Eye*, took to calling Tony the "royal photographer of restricted growth." The fact of the matter is that Tony is quite short, standing five-feet six-inches tall. Of course, this means he is five inches taller than Princess Margaret, whom certain acquaintances say Tony referred to late in their marriage as "the dwarf." The fact is that, slight of build or not, Tony was a very presentable young man who had no trouble whatsoever making his mark on society.

In 1951, the young photographer got a job with a court photographer who was also a personal friend of Prince Philip's from wartime days. Several months later, Tony opened his own studio, and he began gradually building a following and a reputation for himself as a very talented photographer.

It was in 1956 that Antony Armstrong-Jones's connection with the royal family began in earnest. He had met the duke of Kent and wrote to him requesting a sitting. The duke agreed, liked the pictures, and asked Tony to do his twenty-first birthday portrait. With one royal door opened, others were soon to follow, and after that initial bit of success, Tony was soon getting as much work as he could handle.

Tony was not only talented—he was also very sociable. He loved going out and was at ease immediately in any crowd. With his amazingly active social life, it was astounding to some people that Tony ever got any work done at all. He was always on the go, attending parties, always with a beautiful woman on his arm. He was part of London's hippest crowd, a melange of sophisticated, moneyed, liberated people. In Tony's group, free love was accepted with nary a raised eyebrow, careers were invariably artistic, and all sorts of people—from heiresses to homosexuals to hangers-on—mixed and mingled. He was definitely one of the *avant-garde*.

The *avant-garde* was, naturally, what Margaret had always been seeking. There was no man more her match than Tony, who had once assured an acquaintance, "The spur of the moment is the essence of adventure."

The "essence of adventure" had led Tony into many a liaison in his day. His ex-girlfriends included Henrietta Tiarks, the daughter of multimillionaire banker Henry Tiarks; Edwina Carroll, an Anglo-Burmese actress; and Jackie Chan, a breathtakingly beautiful half-Chinese actress-dancer.

Tony's relationship with Jackie was the most serious of all these linkings. She had known the photographer for three years when his engagement to Margaret was announced, and it had been generally accepted that she and Tony were a very serious item. She gave strength to this rumor when she went into hiding after he'd announced his betrothal to another. And she later had the ironic distinction of playing Gwenny Lee, the Japanese "yum-yum girl" who never gets her man, in the film version of *The World of Suzie Wong*.

Like Margaret, Tony was a born romantic as opposed to a practical realist. He once admitted to a close friend, "I believe that a man only really falls in love once. When that happened, I'd marry the girl—whoever she was!" Little did he imagine at the time who that girl would turn out to be!

Margaret got to know Tony through the efforts of her close friend Elizabeth Cavendish. Elizabeth was, like Margaret, agog at the theatrical world and very friendly with the artistic class. She brought Margaret to a rehearsal of John Crank's revue, *Cranks*, in 1956. Elizabeth was a backer of the show and wanted Margaret's opinion of certain aspects of it. The "front of the house" photographs for the revue were being taken by Antony Armstrong-Jones, but Margaret didn't meet him just then.

When Margaret did get a chance to sit and talk at length with Tony, she liked what she heard and saw. The occasion was a dinner party in February of 1957, given by Elizabeth Cavendish at her mother's house at 5 Cheyne Walk in Chelsea. By then, Tony was well established as a photographer. He was doing a lot of work for *Vogue*, as he

141

still does, and he had recently shot a study of Princess Anne and Prince Charles at Buckingham Palace. Now he and Princess Margaret were discovering an immediate rapport.

At the time, Tony was living in Pimlico Road, where he had a combination of studio and living quarters between an antique shop and a laundry. It was no tacky artist's workshop, but a stylish flat which he had decorated tastefully himself and which even boasted an all-white sitting room with candelabra-type wall lamps.

Tony and Margaret's courtship did not develop in this studio, but in a small, run-down flat at 59 Rotherhithe Street, across the Thames by the Deptford ferry. The apartment, which Tony and Margaret always referred to as "the Room," belonged to William Glenton, a journalist friend of Tony's, who had loaned it to the photographer.

The Room, in a building which has since been razed, was no Buckingham Palace. It lived up to its nickname, consisting of a twelve-foot square area with rush mats on the floor, bentwood chairs, an ancient couch and an assortment of junkshop curios for decoration.

This was where the courtship of Antony Armstrong-Jones and Her Royal Highness Princess Margaret took place. It was a secret courtship which many felt was motivated by Margaret's desire to "get even" with those who had pressured her to break up with Peter Townsend. Tony was a study in ambiguity as far as his marital acceptability was concerned. He was considered suitable, but he still lacked the desirable aristocratic establishment credentials. He was a possible match for Margaret, but not a particularly plausible one.

But it was this man Princess Margaret would fall in love with and choose to marry. It was this man who would father her two children and appear to make her idyllically happy for a while. It was this man who would become a cuckold in the eyes of the world when the princess's dalliance with Roddy Llewellyn on the beaches of Mustique leapt onto the front pages of the world's scandal sheets.

Chapter Eleven

"I will never marry a man who cannot laugh easily," Princess Margaret once confessed, and in Antony Armstrong-Jones, she had certainly found a man with a sense of humor. He had as attractive and magnetic a personality as she could have hoped to find in all of England.

The young Armstrong-Jones—who was thirty, like Margaret, when they married—was witty, personable and intelligent. He was well liked by Margaret's circle, and even the hard-to-please Queen Mother considered him a breath of fresh air. After Tony went to tea with Margaret and her mum at Clarence House, he was given the seal of approval—but he was approved of as an escort, not necessarily as a husband.

The truth was that Margaret was more or less

on the market. It was inconceivable that she should pass her thirtieth year without a husband; that would catapult her straight into British spinsterhood. And it wasn't as if Margaret would be clutching at straws were she to marry Tony. Even now, with the marriage over, the general consensus among their friends is that Margaret was deeply in love with Antony Armstrong-Jones when she decided to become his bride.

During their courting days in the Room at Rotherhithe, Margaret and Tony kept their developing relationship a secret from all but a few people. Not even William Glenton, landlord of the Room, was aware that the woman he occasionally spotted visiting the photographer, clad in a nondescript trenchcoat and a headscarf was, in fact, the sister of the queen.

One of the few people who was in on the secret was Billy Wallace, an old and dear friend of Margaret's with whom she had once been linked romantically. "I've never seen two people so happy," was Billy's comment when news of the romance leaked out.

Their happiness didn't always influence others into doting on them. In one instance, Tony was commissioned to take Margaret's twenty-ninth birthday portrait. He came up with several pictures that were acceptable, but the public was very negative about the one Margaret liked best. This was a stark black and white portrait that showed Margaret half in shadow, posed with wooden carrousel horses. Margaret loved the picture because she felt, and rightfully so, that Tony had captured something very special about her. But others thought his *Vogue*-ish approach and stylistic tricks were a smidgen too "pop" for royalty.

In the meantime, it was only natural that the romance should progress slowly. Margaret had her own work and responsibilities, and Tony certainly had his. Their lives were active, and both frequently had business away from London.

Since her father's death—even in the midst of her inner turmoil over her involvement with Peter Townsend—Margaret had paid strict attention to the requirements of her station. She threw herself into all her official duties with a smile, and during her courtship with Tony, one of these official duties was a great deal of traveling.

Shortly after she began seeing Tony, Margaret was off to the Caribbean, for her second tour of the Islands. She was growing quite fond of these luxurious, expense-paid state visits and of the opportunities they provided to see the rest of the world. "How well traveled I am becoming!" she enthused after returning from this Caribbean junket. "When people now talk to me of Scarborough, my mind turns less naturally to the North Riding than to Tobago."

These trips were not all fun and games, of course. There were many public functions to attend, dignitaries to meet, tours to make. It was as much work as it was play. "One tries to behave informally, of course, within the formal framework," Margaret once explained in reference to her travels. "One enjoys that, most of the time. It's important to give pleasure to other people."

Giving pleasure to others sometimes meant dragging oneself to a tiresome fancy dress ball when one's head felt as if it were splitting right open from migraine. But it could also mean eating the best food and drinking the finest wine, staying in the poshest places and meeting the most interesting people in every stop along the way.

Not long after her Caribbean tour, Margaret was off again, this time on a trip to Canada. But even her journeys couldn't keep her affection for Armstrong-Jones from flowering. They continued to meet in the Room at Rotherhithe, continued to get to know each other, continued to be in love.

Margaret admired Tony's industriousness and talent. She had always been drawn to those with artistic talents, especially if those people, like Tony, had entrée to the world of show business and were on good terms with the most fashionable people in the world.

Coming from such a lonely, withdrawn background herself, Margaret was duly impressed when she learned that Tony's polio had kept him confined to a wheelchair for a year of his childhood. She admired his indomitable spirit. Though Tony was more adept socially and much more extroverted than Margaret could ever attempt to be, Tony was also sensitive and understanding. Moreover, he always treated her with the deference due a royal princess.

But was Antony Armstrong-Jones the husband due a royal princess? That was the question, and the answer appeared to be no. It was another of those betwixt and between situations. The royal family wanted Margaret to marry, but they would have been a great deal happier had she chosen someone other than Antony Armstrong-Jones, who was well-connected enough for a commoner but really not of their class. And yet, no one wanted to deny Margaret yet another chance at happiness. The Peter Townsend affair was still fresh enough in everyone's mind.

The decision finally to announce Margaret's engagement to Tony was not reached without some degree of tension. Once, while walking pensively away from a family conference at Buckingham Palace, Margaret told a friend, "This is *their* Battle of Jutland." As far as she was concerned, she had given in to pressure once and ditched the man she loved. She wasn't going to be a two-time loser.

Even during their dating days, there was evidence that a wee undercurrent of sarcasm was already present in Margaret and Tony's relationship. For instance, he affectionately called her "Pet" and "Sweetness," while her nickname for him was "Tiresome," a grim portent of the petty bitterness to come.

The first thing to come, though, was of a pleasant sort. It was an announcement, on February 26, 1960, of the engagement of Princess Margaret and Antony Armstrong-Jones. To give the two lovers official approval, genealogists at Debrett's and Burke's Peerage had worked overtime to come up with the revelation that Tony was actually the twenty-first grandson (which is to say the great-great-great-great-etcetera) of King Edward I, and also Margaret's twelfth cousin twice removed. He was also the first male commoner to marry into the royal family in five hundred years, the last having been Owen Tudor, who married Catherine, the widow of Henry V.

Due to the palace's propensity for handing out titles to those who married into the royal midst, Tony gained a title as well as a wife, although it wasn't bestowed upon him until after he and Margaret had been wed a year and the princess was expecting her first child. At that time, the queen conferred an earldom upon Tony, who would henceforth be known as the earl of Snowdon, with the subsidiary title, requisite to a first-born son, of Viscount Linley of Nymans. Margaret could then be known by the title Princess Margaret, the countess of Snowdon, as opposed to being just plain Mrs. Armstrong-Jones.

She became Mrs. Armstrong-Jones at enormous expense. Ministry of Work funds to the tune of $56,000 were spent under the direction of Lord John Hope in preparation for the celebration. This amount provided $8,500 just for fresh spring flowers!

Announcement of the engagement was put off until after Queen Elizabeth II gave birth to her third child, a son. Prince Andrew was born February 19, 1960, and it was just a week later that the evening media programs were interrupted for another all-important announcement.

"It is with great pleasure," it decreed, "that Queen Elizabeth the Queen Mother announces the betrothal of her beloved daughter The Princess Margaret to Mr. Antony Charles Robert Armstrong-Jones, son of Mr. R.O.L. Armstrong-Jones, Q.C., and the countess of Rosse, to which union The Queen has gladly given her consent."

Before the wedding, Margaret and Tony had much to do, including searching out a place to live. Tony was in the process of getting rid of his Pimlico studio (now a big tourist attraction) through a private sale, and the queen had graciously offered her future brother-in-law the use of a first floor suite at Buckingham Palace. The queen, who may not have been overjoyed at the prospect of Margaret's upcoming marriage but wouldn't have dreamt of being ungracious about it, also arranged for the Crown Estate Commissioners to show the engaged couple an available space at Number 10 Kensington Palace.

Kensington Palace is actually a series of townhouses, set back off the Kensington High Street and surrounded by quiet gardens and the London Museum. Princess Alexandra and her husband, Angus Ogilvy, are currently other residents in the palace, where Margaret and Tony were granted a grace-and-favor lease for their first home.

The wedding date was set for the sixth of May. A ring was being fashioned for Margaret of the same Welsh gold that had supplied Elizabeth II's wedding band. There was still enough gold left, after Margaret's ring was finished, for one more ring. And so this special gold, which had been a gift to the Little Princesses when they were young, made three royal wedding rings—one for Lilibet, one for Margaret, and one for Princess Anne when she married Mark Phillips. Margaret's engagement ring was interesting in itself, and it testifies once more to Tony's total originality and uniqueness. The ring had a large ruby, set within a ring of smaller diamonds. It was beautiful.

Also beautiful was the gown Norman Hartnell designed for the occasion, a gown which created great excitement when sketches of it appeared in *Women's Wear Daily* before the wedding, much to the dismay and anger of the princess. Happily for Margaret, who wanted her dress to be a surprise, most advance reports got the details wrong, so there was still an element of surprise when she walked down the aisle at Westminster Abbey.

The dress was very simple, with long sleeves, a full skirt, and a flowing train. For bridesmaids, Margaret chose eight children, none older than eight. Besides her niece Princess Anne, she was attended by Catherine Vesey, Virginia Fitzroy, Angela Nevill, Sarah Lowther, Annabel Rhodes, Rose Nevill and Marilyn Wills.

Those thousands of dollars worth of flowers

weren't wasted. At the top of the Mall, an arch of roses stood sixty feet high. Banners bearing the initials of the bride and groom flew from masts which lined the way to Westminster Abbey.

Some would call Margaret's wedding ceremony a circus. Certainly it was the first time television cameras had ever recorded a British royal wedding—even though the two "stars" would allow no close-ups of themselves during their actual vows.

Outside the Abbey, a quarter of a million Britons lined the processional route, cheering and singing wildly, "For He's a Jolly Good Fellow" when Tony exited with his bride. One notable who didn't appear all that jolly was the queen. Lilibet sat glum and strained-looking throughout her little sister's wedding ceremony, perking up only much later when, following the wedding breakfast at Buckingham Palace, the royal family pelted the newlyweds with confetti and rose petals. Then the queen melted; her smile flashed as brightly as everyone else's as she tossed petals at Margaret and Tony. Deep down, she wished very much that her sister would make a satisfying life for herself.

The queen wasn't the only one with ambivalent feelings about Tony. It seemed as if everyone *liked* him, but no one was certain if he was quite *right* for Princess Margaret.

However, Mrs. Anna Garnett, mother of Tony's close friend Andy Garnett, was sure the bride and groom would be perfectly content.

"Tony has wonderful ideas on decoration," she gushed. "Bright colors, goldfish bowls in the walls—anything. Princess Margaret's home and his will be the chicest in London."

Besides the fact that it takes more than good decorating to make a marriage work, there were others who felt that no degree of chic would be enough to keep the couple from dealing with reality. Tony's seventy-two-year-old charlady was one who viewed the union with a more jaundiced eye. "Princess Margaret may have to change her ways," Mrs. Ethel Wright remarked, "but she isn't the only one. She will have to persuade Mr. Armstrong-Jones to be tidier. Maybe he was busy, but he used to let the place get into an awful mess."

Tidiness could wait until after the honeymoon. Margaret and Tony were waved away on the royal yacht *Britannia* for a five-week cruise to the West Indies. This was no Arthur Frommer budget vacation, either, considering that it cost $112,000 for the ship to be manned by twenty officers and 237 sailors. Small wonder there was some public outcry about wasteful spending after the wedding excitement had died down!

The cruise was a long game of hide and seek with photographers and reporters who took every opportunity to spy on the honeymooners. The exact island destinations were a carefully guarded secret, but that didn't keep magazines and press agencies from covering *all* of the Caribbean Islands with lensmen and then just sitting back and waiting for the princess and her groom to show up anywhere in the vicinity.

Some of the places were swamped with well-wishers and fans when the couple arrived. Other days, the ship would pull into tiny coves or quiet lagoons to drop off the couple for several hours of privacy. "It was so very wonderful for both of us," Margaret later said, "just to lie on those deserted beaches, without a soul in sight. Neither of us ever wanted to be rescued in the evening and we would have gladly lived in a little grass hut."

One very interesting event that took place during their honeymoon was a brief visit to the island in the Grenadines owned by their friends Colin and Anne Tennant. When Margaret and Tony came ashore, the Tennants were waiting to greet them, along with a few other friends and Tony's uncle, Oliver Messel. The Tennants owned the entire island and were planning to develop it. At the time, however, it was very rustic. When the newlyweds came ashore, the Tennants were pleased to present them with a very special wedding gift—a parcel of secluded beachfront land.

It was a perfectly wonderful present, and Margaret and Tony were very excited about it. They later built a house there, helped along by the striking designs of Tony's Uncle Oliver. The Armstrong-Joneses passed many happy weeks on this tiny island over the years. Eventually, however, as their union weakened, Tony stopped going there while Margaret continued to spend time there alone. Eventually, Margaret would no longer be spending her time on the island alone. The honeymoon gift was acreage on the isle of Mustique, and that's where Margaret took Roddy Llewellyn and set in motion the chain of events that would end her marriage.

Chapter Twelve

The early years of marriage were truly happy ones for Tony and Margaret. This was a period when they were both at their best. They were like any other newlyweds in their enthusiasm to settle into their new home, and they were understandably proud of their own accomplishments at getting it all together.

Number 10 Kensington Palace had been pretty run-down when Margaret and Tony discovered it. But together, they fixed it up and made it a charming abode, displaying the kind of zest only a couple moving into their first home can muster. Tony was very clever with his hands and had always loved fixing up old houses—in his studio in Pimlico, there was a staircase he had even built himself. Now, under his guidance and with the help of the modern carpentry workshop he had installed, Margaret found that she enjoyed being a craftswoman. Her pride and joy was a large pair of carved doors that she and Tony had made themselves. The woman who had been so proud of her cooking and cleaning skills as a Little Princess with her little Welsh cottage now showed the same kind of pride as she viewed her handiwork and showed it off to visitors.

As young marrieds, Margaret and Tony were as romantic a pair as could be found outside a movie screen. They even made a nostalgic journey back to the Room in Rotherhithe with a bag of groceries one evening, to dine together in the same space where they had fallen in love and begun their life together.

"It's one of the sweetest rooms I know," Margaret said of Rotherhithe. "It's made us so happy." And those who remember her as a young bride recall that she was happiest then, especially when she and Tony could lock themselves away in that magical Room. There, she no longer had to worry about behaving like a princess, no longer had to think of protocol or propriety. In the Room, as in the Little House of her childhood, Margaret was no longer royalty, no longer a personage. She was just a person, just another woman in love with her man.

Still, the Room in Rotherhithe, with its chipped enamel sink, rickety couch and rush mats on the floor, had little to do with real life, the real life of a princess and her husband.

Of course, at that time, the real life of Tony and Margaret was still very blissful, especially so when Margaret found she was pregnant. The announcement of the news to the queen brought an offer of larger living space. The queen asked Margaret and Tony if they would like the larger apartments at Number One A Kensington Palace. The renovation of this building, much damaged during the war, would take almost two years to complete. But as soon as the restoration was finished, Margaret and Tony moved in, along with their son, David Albert Charles, Viscount Linley of Nymans, born November 3, 1961.

The princess chose to have her baby at home, but on the advice of her doctors, she agreed to have the delivery at the better-equipped Clarence House instead. By the time her daughter, Lady Sarah Frances Elizabeth, came along, Margaret was ensconced in her new quarters at 1a Kensington Palace, which had been renovated— much to the public's displeasure—at a cost of 85,000 pounds.

Much has been written about Princess Margaret's being either a good mother or a bad mother, with both sides usually offering up suitable material for an argument. The theory that Princess Margaret takes motherhood less than seriously was undoubtedly begun when she and Tony took off for an island vacation when their baby son was just two months old. They left David with the Queen Mother and his nanny to soak in the sun at Antigua, a leavetaking which wasn't considered in keeping with a loving new mother.

But for Margaret, getting away alone with her husband may have seemed a stark necessity at the time. Postpartum blues are common enough, and, in Margaret's case, she had good reason to feel blue. After all, she and Tony hadn't been married long before he'd started admitting to friends, "It's a damn bore being married to one person." Now she wanted to be as exciting and attractive as she could be for him—not his child's mother or a young matron, but a tanned, sexy mistress frolicking on the sand. This wasn't an isolated holiday—just a few months after the birth of Lady Sarah, Margaret and Tony were off alone again, on another island interlude.

A quiet life of mundane monogamy had never been Tony's idea of a good time, and now he began devoting more and more time to his burgeoning career. He accepted a position as an artistic advisor to the Sunday *Times* in addition to his regular work for the queen with the Council of Industrial Design.

When did problems start cropping up in Margaret and Tony's marriage? And why? It wasn't just that Tony began resenting having his wings clipped. It was also difficult for him to happily comply with all the official, obsequious rules—like having to walk four paces behind his wife when entering a public place. "My husband has made me twice the person I used to be," Margaret reportedly told one close friend during the early years of their marriage, but perhaps for Tony, twice wasn't enough. After all, he was used to being surrounded by top professional women. Margaret's profession was being a princess, but other than being able to give speeches and attend public functions, that took no special skills or artistic talents

Antony Armstrong-Jones was no weak-willed dilettante who had seen his chance to latch onto something good. He was a man of strong will, great ambition, much talent, and a hot temper. He liked the notoriety of being married to a princess, but at the same time, he had no intentions of bowing down to a sense of outmoded convention or being tied to royal apron strings.

Tony had his share of fine points, and the desire to be a docile consort to a princess wasn't one of them. Lady Lewisham said a lot about the strong force of Tony's personality nearly two decades ago when she recalled an incident between the two of them. "I have known Tony all my life," she said. "He was a terribly handsome little boy. I remember once I was at René the hairdresser's and Tony was taking advertising pictures. He caught me under the hairdryer. My hair was wet and in curlers. He said, 'Let me take a picture of you like that. It won't appear anywhere.' He'd practically taken it already by then. The next thing I knew, it was in a national newspaper. My husband was horrified, but Tony talked me out of being angry. He said, 'It was good. It was real. I honestly didn't think you'd mind.' Tony isn't a society type. He doesn't like coming-out balls and things like that."

He *did* like being married to a princess, but he seemed to like the privileges and power less when the novelty wore off. And, as the novelty wore off, the pressure was laid on. The palace—that vague appellation which always means the queen and sometimes implies the added pressure of Prince Philip, the Queen Mother or other "advisors"—made it perfectly clear that life would be a lot more pleasant for all concerned if Tony would just try to lead a more conservative life. Bohemian lifestyles were fine—in films or on the stage. In the royal family, they had no place.

Trying to persuade Tony to lead a quiet life was like trying to persuade a Southern Baptist he should worship Mecca. Not only does he feel adamant about refusing, he doesn't see the point of it all in the first place. After all, *his* choice of a path isn't harming anyone, so what difference does it all make?

Tony Armstrong-Jones didn't marry Princess Margaret under any guises. He presented himself to the princess and the rest of the royal family just as he was—a socially connected photographer who was ambitious and gregarious, who respected the monarchy but who was happier hanging out with his own crowd of friends. He bent over backwards to do his bit—to accompany his wife to the necessary state functions, to serve the throne, to be a loyal subject. But he wouldn't allow anything to interfere with his work or his friends. As far as he was concerned, being a member of royalty was his wife's job. His own was being a photographer.

As in most marriages, the erosion was gradual. And, with the passage of time, not only did the marriage itself change, but the husband and wife changed as well. Unfortunately, neither the husband, the wife nor the union itself was to change for the best.

Tony tried to toe the line and to be the proper princess's husband, but it was difficult. He didn't want to mix much with the royal set—he missed his artist friends. And yet, when he went back to his old crowd, he would often feel just as out of place.

Being married to a member of the royal family, Tony was fast discovering, had drawbacks aplenty. There was tension in many situations, such as the evening when Tony was having a drink with some friends and another old acquaintance entered the pub and approached him. "Oh, hello, Tony," the fellow addressed him. "How is the old girl—given you the night off, has she?"

His pride wounded, his quick temper piqued, Tony retorted in anger, "If you are referring to Princess Margaret, she is in the best of health, thank you." The silence that ensued was long enough and awkward enough to remind Tony that he no longer fit in with his old gang.

Tony now fit in nowhere. He didn't get along particularly well with any of his royal in-laws, being on cool terms with the queen and like oil and water with Prince Philip. Now Tony attempted to ease Princess Margaret more into his own crowd, only to discover that her regal attitude gave most of his friends a royal pain. So he and the princess became social castaways, only to discover that clinging to each other offered little comfort indeed.

To relieve his disenchantment, Tony threw himself into fixing up yet another ramshackle abode, the "Old House," a building on the grounds of one of his mother's homes, in Sussex. Margaret wasn't particularly interested in spending much time there, and the cottage eventually became known as Tony's "love nest," since everyone took for granted that it was here that he met his girlfriends after he and Margaret started getting along badly.

How to beat the creeping boredom and discontent, that was the question. In 1965, a visit to the United States was scheduled for Margaret and Tony. The princess had hopes that her official visit would prove a pleasant journey for herself and her husband, a chance for them to be close again. It was a pleasant trip—but only for the royal couple. Other Britons were up in arms about the visit, which ended up costing the Foreign Office a record $90,000 for thirty days. If Margaret wanted to combine an "official" trip with an unofficial second honeymoon, that was her business, but her need to travel with an entourage of eleven, including a hairdresser, two personal maids, two secretaries and a lady-in-waiting, didn't set well with the folks back home, the folks who were footing the bill with their tax monies.

As they were forced to become more and more dependent on each other to make their marriage work, the princess and Tony became less charming, less kind, less witty. It was almost as if, in trying to cement their marriage, they succeeded only in depleting one another.

At one point during the American tour, President Lyndon Johnson proposed a toast at a White House dinner and told Lord Snowdon, "I have learned only two things are necessary to keep one's wife happy. First, let her think she is having her own way. Second, let her have it."

With Her Royal Highness Princess Margaret, Tony had no choice. She was used to having her own way, and fighting that was an uphill struggle for her husband. There was, for example, the time Tony tried to perk up Margaret's appearance, only to realize finally that she was going to end up wearing what she wanted to wear, no matter how awful she might actually look in the clothes.

In adulthood, Margaret began displaying in earnest the family legacy of dowdiness. She had her own ideas about what was fashionable, and these were usually formed without giving any consideration to the Hanoverian dimensions of her own figure.

Margaret has a squat little body. She is tiny and

small-boned, with a tendency towards overweight and a large, dowager's bosom. Unfortunately for her appearance, Margaret does little to minimize her bad points, wearing dresses that emphasize her pouter pigeon bustline and skirt lengths that call undue attention to her fat little legs. In 1970, Margaret was scored by the press for trying to wear the chic tall girl's midiskirt—in which she looked like a "a little plump dump." For the wife of a famed fashion photographer to dress this way was beyond the pale. Margaret knew absolutely nothing about the basic rule of fashion: which is to wear what enhances one, not what's in style at the time.

Tony did his best to try to alleviate Margaret's dowdy, comical appearance, and to lead her away from the likes of Hardy Amies and Norman Hartnell. But his plan to modernize Margaret was thwarted by no less than the lady herself when one designer chosen by Tony asked the princess if she was seeking something for her public or private life. "I am always in public," was Margaret's lofty reply, thereby ending *that* discussion and leaving little room for adventure in wardrobe design.

Margaret and Tony were rapidly losing all popularity with the masses. Her snippy attitude, in addition to their consumption of funds, was not well received. Nor were many people crazy about what they considered the Armstrong-Joneses' lack of royal manners. When Margaret and Tony arrived late at the Cannes Film Festival after having kept the assembly waiting for their arrival, they were soundly booed. It was a new low in their steady decline.

By this time, rumors regarding the Snowdons' marriage were rampant. And the rumors were all to the same effect—that the union was on the rocks. Upon hearing this report, the princess remarked, "Wish there were rocks. Our marriage is in the mud." She was making a joking reference to the muck and tractors then surrounding the Old House in Sussex, which Tony was in the process of renovating. But some could feel the strain behind her sense of humor. They knew that her marriage to Tony *was* in the mud and the mire.

In the meantime, polite London society was splitting into two camps—those who whispered that the marriage was definitely in trouble, and those loyal friends of either Margaret or Tony who continued to back up the couple in their denials of any breach.

At this point, Margaret and Tony could still convince a few friends that they were happy. But time was running out. It wouldn't be very long before neither Tony nor Margaret bothered to keep up much of a front any longer, before their public quarrels and other liaisons were dividing their acquaintances into yet another two camps. This time, their friends would be split as to who deserved to bear the blame for this fairytale marriage having turned into the classic nightmare of love gone sour.

Chapter Thirteen

The Armstrong-Jones marriage reached a state of ruin with startling alacrity. The ruin wasn't brought about by Margaret's eventual island tête-à-tête with Roddy Llewellyn or by their clandestine meetings at his British commune. No, that was really quite an anticlimax for the royal couple. Margaret and Tony's marriage by then had been so bad for so long that the Llewellyn incident was thought of as no more than the very last straw.

By the time Margaret and Tony finally got around to asking the queen to sanction a legal separation, the marriage had been spiritually—and *notoriously*—over for several years. They had had hideous quarrels before: Roddy Llewellyn was *not* the first third party being named in the union; there had been more "outsiders" mentioned in connection with the Armstrong-Jones marriage over the years than there were pence in the pound.

The spats between Margaret and Tony were legendary. After one of their first major quarrels, Tony had simply picked up and disappeared with nary a word. When he didn't show up at home again, Margaret had tearfully telephoned all around town asking if anyone happened to have seen her husband. When Tony had been gone a week without getting in touch with her, Margaret swallowed her pride and confessed his desertion to her sister. Tony returned to his wife on his own, but by then the damage had been done. Margaret was humiliated, and Tony was simply furious that she'd dragged her family into their private life.

It was around this time that Tony started spending lengthy periods at the Old House in Sussex—minus his spouse—and that his name started being linked with the names of several very attractive women.

One of those who was reportedly an item with Lord Snowdon was Lady Jacqueline Rufus Isaacs, then just twenty-four and the daughter of a Sussex neighbor, the marquess of Reading. She denied any romance, but she couldn't deny that she had been the one to faithfully visit Tony when he was at a London clinic for minor surgery—whereas his wife didn't show up for any visits until after the romance rumors between Tony and Jacqui had made the papers.

So Jacqui faded out, but the problems in the

Snowdon domicile remained. Tony's friends insisted that Margaret was too jealous of all of Tony's acquaintances, male and female. She was, they said, like a jealous cat, following Tony around at parties, keeping a possessive eye on him, fending off any unwanted attention he might be receiving—attention unwanted by Margaret, that is.

There was also Margaret's notorious bitchiness to contend with. Her personality had become a more pronounced dichotomy of "plain old Maggie" and the Royal Princess. And it was often difficult to choose which was harder to bear.

The "royal" side popped up at the oddest times. It had always been that way. One acquaintance recalled enquiring after King George VI's health as far back as the early 1950s. In asking Margaret how the king was feeling, the friend had referred to him as "your father." Margaret just glared and asked icily, "I presume you mean His Majesty?" She was always quick to put a peon in his place.

Another example of Margaret's holier-than-thou attitude was recalled by a host at a country house party. Weary of Tony and Margaret's constant bickering in front of his other guests, the host asked Margaret if she minded if he retired early, adding that everyone else could stay up and dance and drink as long as they liked. Instead of graciously bidding her thoughtful host a good night, Margaret offered a rebuke. "You *know* you shouldn't—until I do so!" she haughtily informed the man.

That's one side of Margaret, a side few liked. But no one was wild about her concept of friendliness, either. As her relationship with Tony continued to deteriorate, Margaret's need to hear the worst about everyone else continued to flower. She once greeted a close friend by saying, "Tell me all the latest dirt. You know I love to hear wicked things about people."

Most of the wicked things she was hearing happened to be about Tony.

Pamela Colin, a London editor of *Vogue* magazine (who would later marry Jackie Kennedy's former beau, Lord Harlech), kept company with Tony for a time, and it was her friendship with him that first brought Margaret to the brink of divorce.

Margaret was docile at first; Pamela Colin's name appeared on the guest list for all Kensington Palace social events. Then it all got to be too much for Margaret, supposedly because Tony had failed to show up at a special luncheon for the queen and had been discovered with Miss Colin instead. Margaret could deal with slights to her own person, but where her sister was concerned, she was easily made distraught.

So Margaret, furious at her husband's insult to the queen, informed the royal family of her marital situation in all its seamy depth. On December 18, 1967, a meeting was held at Buckingham Palace. In attendance were the queen, Prince Philip, the Queen Mother, Princess Margaret and Lord Snowdon. The discussion centered around the most dire of all topics— whether or not Margaret and Tony should divorce.

There was a precedent for a legal breakup, since Lord Harewood had been permitted to divorce his wife. But it wasn't thát simple. Margaret still loved Tony, and Tony himself wasn't ready to give up his place in the royal family. The duke of Edinburgh would have been happy to have Tony out, the Queen Mother was heartbroken over the whole situation, and the queen wanted—above anything—to avoid any more scandal. She suggested that Tony and Margaret try to keep their union from totally falling apart at the seams, even if that meant going their own separate ways from that time on.

And so, for the most part, that's exactly what they did. When Tony and Margaret did appear together in public, everyone knew there was bound to be trouble. At a party given by the marquess and marchioness of Dufferin and Ava in 1970, both Margaret and Tony showed up wearing too much makeup. They then proceeded to spend the entire evening glaring and sniping at each other and making everyone else dreadfully uncomfortable. But by then, that behavior was par for the course.

At one dinner dance, Tony was off in a small side room chatting with his friends when suddenly Margaret loomed in the doorway, demanding that he go out and dance with her. "Oh, go away. You bore me," he snapped, no longer even bothering to keep up the slightest semblance of affection.

Jointly, Margaret and Tony were picking up a formidable reputation as a pair of royal freeloaders. It wasn't odd for Margaret to telephone the host or hostess of an upcoming party she had heard about and openly invite herself and Tony along. Nor was it considered out of the ordinary for Tony to get in touch with this or that acquaintance who owned a beach home or other pleasant hideaway and ask if it was all right if he and Margaret popped by to visit for a week or so. They were, not surprisingly, a less than popular couple.

In the late 1960s, even Margaret's close and lasting friendship with Sharman Douglas, the former U.S. ambassador's daughter, reached an unpleasant end. Margaret and Tony had agreed to appear as guests of honor at a charity ball that Sharman, now Mrs. Andrew Hay, was throwing in New York City. The ball was a financial failure and Mrs. Hay couldn't come up with the $30,000 Margaret had demanded as a fee for her appearance.

Today her ex-friend Sharman says, "I still miss her friendship terribly, and I refuse to say any but the nicest things about her. To me, she is still one of the most remarkable women in the world. Every year since that happened I've sent her a Christmas card which she never answers. Whenever I'm in London, I invite her for cocktails. She never responds. I still think I'll be able to get her friendship back someday. After all, $30,000 shouldn't be too hard to raise. . . ." That's the high price of friendship with Princess Margaret.

In the meantime, Tony's eye kept wandering and his name continued to be linked—with this fashion model, with that socialite, even with actress Gayle Hunnicutt. But now Tony wasn't the only one doing his own thing. Margaret was doing hers as well.

In addition to acquiring a hearty appetite for gin and tonics, Margaret was also busily pursuing her own version of the social merry-go-round. She was seen night after night, out on the town, chain-smoking her strong French cigarettes, in the company of such men as Patrick, Lord Litchfield; Dominic Eliott, the divorced son of the earl of Minto; or television executive Derek Hart. So often was Margaret seen with Peter Sellers during this time (his own marriage to Britt Ekland was then on the skids) that the couple was greeted by Sellers' buddy Spike Milligan upon entering Ronnie Scott's nightclub in Soho with the words, "Mr. Peter Sellers, wherever you are, wherever you be, please take your hand off the princess's knee!"

Tony wasn't laughing.

He certainly didn't laugh over the Robin Douglas-Home fiasco. The young man, a nephew of former Prime Minister Sir Alec Douglas-Home and a neurotic playboy type, fell madly in love with Princess Margaret. There was an awful scene at Kensington Palace one night when Tony came home unexpectedly and found Robin there. Tony ordered the young man out of the house, telling him in no uncertain terms never to return.

Things got worse. When Margaret refused to run away with Robin, he committed suicide in his cottage at West Chiltington, Sussex, by taking an overdose of sleeping pills. A stack of love letters was found in his house, from Princess Margaret and written on royal notepaper, all leaving nothing to the imagination.

The letters surfaced in New York, where a private party was attempting to sell them and where parts of them made the local scandal sheets. But someone, most certainly of the royal family, came to Margaret's rescue. The letters quickly disappeared, undoubtedly disposed of in the royal shredder or incinerator.

Yes, the marriage between Antony Armstrong-Jones and Princess Margaret was certainly going to hell in a handcart, and now, with the Douglas-Home incident a humiliating blow to his own self-respect, it was Tony who wanted a divorce. But the queen still didn't like the idea of a marital failure in her own family. She stalled for time, hoping perhaps that Margaret and Tony would manage to work things out, never dreaming that things could get even worse, that with the advent of Roddy Llewellyn, events would take the most bizarre turn yet, a turn that could lead only to an official end to the marriage that had become a total farce.

Chapter Fourteen

Queen Elizabeth the Queen Mother, one recalls, used to remind her daughters when they were small, "Your work is the rent you pay for the room you occupy on earth." Now Margaret was making a travesty of that heartfelt statement. Work? Margaret was devoting her time exclusively to hedonism, and that self-indulgent attitude was turning public opinion sharply against her.

The monarchy has a responsibility to Great Britain. The royal family lives well, for free, with meaty salaries to boot. Princess Margaret's allowance, as of 1971, was approximately $70,000 a year, and what was she doing to deserve it? Nothing, according to people like Labour M.P. Willie Hamilton, a crusader to end the monarchy. After the Roddy Llewellyn scandal broke,

Hamilton publicly branded Margaret a "parasite."

Margaret's selfish behavior reflected not just on herself, but on the British monarchy in general. The movement afoot to discredit what it considered an antiquated waste of money—the maintenance of a royal family—snatched at Margaret's footloose behavior and pointed out that she was an example of how the monarchy was dragging Britain down.

Keeping a royal family in style doesn't come cheap. Consider the fact that, in 1960, Buckingham Palace was listed as occupying forty-five acres of land, woods, a lake and gardens in the very center of London, and that there were a raft of other grace-and-favor private apartments, including Kensington Palace, besides. At Buckingham Palace, there are six hundred and two rooms with a permanent staff of approximately two hundred and fifty footmen, maids, charwomen, kitchen workers and maintenance men to look after them. During a period of financial decline, where else would Britons naturally look when it came to cutting corners but to the royal family?

And as most Britons tried desperately to battle the rapid fall of the pound and the skyrocketing of prices, Margaret continued to fritter away her time with a rich hippie named Roddy Llewellyn, and she appeared to be having a jolly good time doing just that. Her "Marie Antoinette aroma" had now developed into a full-blown case of what one might term the "let them eat cake" syndrome.

And the "peasants" weren't going for it a bit.

Roddy is the son of Colonel Harry Llewellyn, one of the queen's closest friends. When Margaret, who'd met him years before, was reintroduced to the tall, handsome blond at a party in 1973, she liked what she saw, and she immediately set out to get it.

Get it she did. The handsome hippie, close to twenty years Margaret's junior and affecting a silver earring in his left ear, fell for Margaret as soon as the two met again—which was at a house party arranged by Margaret at her friend Colin Tennant's Glen House in Scotland. Upon returning to London, Roddy gave up working, devoting all his time to Princess Margaret and occasionally picking up unemployment benefits from social security.

It was the queen who first tried to turn the tide of this relationship, by calling upon her old friend, Colonel Harry Llewellyn, Roddy's father. The colonel was furious, and the result was that Roddy fled Europe, taking a train to Turkey and putting up at a cheap hotel until Margaret finally tracked him down and had someone from the British Embassy get him on a plane back to London.

By this time, Roddy was being so pushed and pulled and pressured from all sides that he suffered a nervous breakdown and was for a time a patient at a private clinic in London—where his most loyal visitor was none other than Princess Margaret, to the surprise of no one.

By the time Roddy was released, Margaret was spending most of her time with him. When the two weren't sunning in Mustique or meeting clandestinely at friends' apartments in London, they were at Roddy's commune near Bath, which he operated jointly with several other rich hippie-type friends.

At Surrendell Farm, it was a common sight to see Princess Margaret walking around the forty-seven-acre spread wearing rubber workboots, rugged slacks and an old jacket, sometimes weeding the vegetable patch or just cleaning up. It was just like those childhood days back at the Little House. Only now, instead of playing "let's be middle class," Margaret was playing "let's be poor."

Like Roddy and the seven of his friends who also lived there, Margaret received no special treatment and reportedly dossed down on the floor, on an old mattress, when she spent the night. Lord Snowdon had always been known as the only member of the royal family who mixed with ordinary people in ordinary walks of life. Now Margaret was making up for lost time—but in a way that could hardly be expected to meet with anyone's approval.

Still, if it hadn't been for the photographer who visited Mustique disguised as an ordinary tourist and who snapped those incriminating pictures, Margaret and Tony might still be together today. The queen wanted very much for her sister and Lord Snowdon to stay together; Margaret was amenable, as long as she could live her own life; Tony didn't mind being a member of the royal family as long as he didn't have to mingle with the rest of them. But those snapshots of Margaret and Roddy were too much to dismiss. They propelled Tony into a breakup.

The public humiliation brought down upon Tony's head by those intimate island snapshots was just too much for him to bear. He could stand whatever Margaret did to his pride privately, but when dirty little affairs started spilling over in glaring headlines, that was it.

Tony went to the queen, and on March 17, 1976, the first statement from Buckingham Palace on the splitting up of Princess Margaret and Antony Armstrong-Jones was released.

The statement was brief and simply announced that the royal family had discussed the situation, but that the archbishop of Canterbury, Donald Coggin, had barred comment about any possible divorce or legal separation. The archbishop did admit that he had spoken to the palace on the telephone, but he refused to reveal what decision had been reached. A spokesman for the Church of England admitted that the queen had spoken to the archbishop regarding the possibility of a divorce for Margaret and Tony.

Lord Snowdon, in the meantime, was in Hong Kong, on his way to Sydney, Australia for a major exhibition of his photographs. He had no comment, he informed the reporters who questioned him there. What was there to say? He knew that, as far as the royal family were concerned, it was all his fault, regardless of the fact that it was Margaret who had been caught publicly, while he, Tony, had always been discreet. Until details were ironed out, there was little he could say without risking offending the queen and thereby hurting both his career and his social standing in Great Britain. And, of course, there were the children— Viscount Linley and Lady Sarah—to think about. They had gone through enough already.

By the next day, the queen had talked with lawyers concerning Margaret's marital mess, and it appeared that a legal separation would serve as the immediate answer. Regardless of the outcome, neither a legal separation nor a divorce would affect Margaret's position as fifth in line of succession to the throne nor, presumably, would either affect her $70,000 income from the queen's privy purse.

On March 19, a brief statement was issued from Kensington Palace to the effect that Margaret and Tony had agreed to live apart and that Margaret would continue to carry out her public duties and functions without him. A spokesman for the queen said she was "very sad at what has happened," and that there was no pressure from her on Margaret and Tony to take any particular course. That was the official word. The unofficial gossip was that Margaret had been told in no uncertain terms to start toeing the line as far as her duties and responsibilities were concerned and also that there was no way

Margaret would ever be allowed to marry Roddy Llewellyn, even if she was granted a divorce from Tony.

A divorce, of course, was considered to be the ultimate outcome of this marriage. Margaret today continues to live at Kensington Palace with her children, while Tony is in the process of buying a house in Kensington which was quoted on the market at approximately $140,000. Two years after the date of their legal separation, Margaret and Tony will be free to divorce with the consent of each other. After five years, a divorce by either one will be possible without the other's consent.

Who was most upset by the breakup? If Tony wasn't, he at least had the good sense to appear to be. Margaret, on the evening before the split was announced, was still out "gallivanting" around. She was in London, attending the film *Butley* at the Curzon Cinema in Mayfair. Interestingly enough, *Butley*, starring Alan Bates, was the story of a man whose offensive self-destructive attitude had ruined his marriage and alienated even those who cared for him most.

In Uganda, President Idi Amin grabbed the chance to make a statement and said that Lord Snowdon's "experience in marriage will be a lesson to all of us men to be careful not to marry ladies in very high positions." He went on to note that "husbands in such marriages can be summarily dismissed by their wives."

This was total rubbish. Tony certainly was not

in the position of being "dismissed" by anyone, and the photographer well knew it. He bore the weight of the breakup like a true gentleman during the press conference he held in Sydney. Tony said he wanted simply "to pray for the understanding of our two children, to wish Princess Margaret every happiness for her future, and to express with utmost humility my love, admiration and respect I will always have for her sister, mother and indeed her entire family." He added that he was "naturally desperately sad in every way that this had to come."

And so Tony managed to handle this last crisis very well indeed and to remain somewhat on the good side of the throne in doing so. In April of 1976, Margaret and Tony met in public for the first time since their separation on the occasion of the confirmation into the Anglican faith of their son. They later joined the queen and other guests for lunch, and on April 22nd, both were present at the queen's fiftieth birthday celebration at Windsor Castle, to which many had expected Tony would not be invited.

Reconciliation? It's out of the picture. Margaret and Tony have made every adjustment to their separation. As the monarch's only sibling, Margaret has long been expected to carry a great deal of the burden of public appearances and official visits. She slacked off from this in the 1960s and early 1970s, but now, with prodding from her sister, she is doing her share of the work and leading a relatively industrious life.

Roddy Llewellyn is still on the scene, but it's expected that his relationship with the princess will just fade away into eventual obscurity, as it indeed appears to be doing.

Margaret, in the meantime, continues to evince confusion regarding her role in life. No one knows what to expect from her, and she appears not to know what to expect from herself. She has retained her eye for younger men—Roddy was a beginning, not the end—but it's a safe bet that her family would never hear of her marrying *any* man nearly twenty years her junior. She continues to enjoy upper-crust gatherings one moment, and a coterie of artists the next. She runs hot and cold, at best, and even her oldest friends aren't sure when to expect a warm greeting and when to expect a frosty snub.

She was the little girl the whole world loved. She was Margaret Rose, the mischievous imp, the "holy terror" whose Mummy and Papa sometimes found impossible to control, the sprite who would dare her governess to stay angry. "Laugh, Crawfie!" she'd shout, and the answering laughter would tell little Margaret she had won.

And now she's the Imperfect Princess, a weary woman in the midst of a lonely, anxious middle age, looking back on one great love that was doomed from the start and one marriage that began as a fairytale romance and ended as an off-color joke.

Where did it all go wrong?

Or did it ever go right?

If the world must continue to be confronted by those who have everything handed to them on a silver platter while the masses continue to struggle for their supper, then Princess Margaret serves a certain purpose by removing the sting. She is proof to the common people that having it all doesn't necessarily mean a thing. One can be rich and beautiful and even a princess and still end up aging, overweight and unhappy. That's the lesson of Princess Margaret. All her life, Margaret has felt left out, unlucky, an outcast. Her position didn't give her enough privileges—as it did Lilibet—to make up for the way in which it isolated her from real life. Yet as a princess she wanted *better* chances, a *better* life, the *best* of everything.

But being a princess turned out to mean having few real childhood friends except her sister, seeing little of her parents, having to give up the one man she really loved and being partner to a loveless marriage long after the affection had run out. As an adult, Margaret was forced to answer to the propriety of her sister just as, as a child, she had been forced to toe the line for Papa.

And she had never wanted that. She had never wanted to be a good little girl.

She had always known she wasn't perfect, but she hadn't cared. She had settled for something very different as her lot in life. She had chosen a course, a very long time ago when she was just a winsome child, that would be uniquely her own. Princess Margaret had made up her mind that she was going to be someone very special, that she was going to be her own person, that she was going to be a star. She was going to create her own legend of Princess Margaret. She made up her mind that even if there were many, many things she wouldn't be able to do, she was going to make people sit up and take notice of her every day of her life.

And that's exactly what she's always done. In the only way she knows how.

Chronology

1895 — Birth of Albert, Princess Margaret's father

1900 — Birth of Elizabeth Bowes-Lyon, Princess Margaret's mother

1905 — Elizabeth Bowes-Lyon meets Albert at a children's party in London

1917 — British royal family changes surname from Guelph to Windsor

April 26, 1923 — Elizabeth Bowes-Lyon marries Albert, the duke of York

April 21, 1926 — Daugher Elizabeth born to duke and duchess of York

1927 — Duke and duchess of York move into house at 145 Piccadilly

March 7, 1930 — Birth of Antony Armstrong-Jones

April 16, 1930 — Announcement of duchess of York's pregnancy

August 21, 1930 — Princess Margaret born at Glamis Castle in Scotland, 9:22 P.M.

November, 1930 — Prince of Wales is introduced to Wallis Warfield Simpson of Baltimore at country house party

1931 — Duke and duchess of York renovate Royal Lodge at Windsor

1934 — Prince of Wales begins courting Mrs. Simpson

May 6, 1935 — Jubilee Day for King George V and Queen Mary

January 30, 1936 — Death of King George V; Prince of Wales succeeds as King Edward VIII

December 11, 1936 — Broadcast of King Edward VIII's abdication speech from Windsor Castle

May 12, 1937 — Coronation of Albert as King George VI

1939 — Outbreak of World War II; Princess Elizabeth introduced to Prince Philip of Greece at Dartmouth Royal Naval College

September 13, 1940—Buckingham Palace bombed

March, 1941—Group Captain Peter Townsend marries Cecil Rosemary Pawle

August 1, 1944—Peter Townsend joins the royal household as Equerry of Honor

May 6, 1945—Royal family returns to London from Windsor Castle

July 10, 1947—Engagement announced between Princess Elizabeth and Prince Philip of Greece

November 20, 1947—Princess Elizabeth marries Prince Philip

November 14, 1948—Birth of Prince Charles

1948—King George VI's health begins to fail

1949—King George VI undergoes surgery for arteriosclerosis

1950—Peter Townsend promoted to Deputy Master of the Royal Household

August 21, 1950—Birth of Princess Anne

1951—Antony Armstrong-Jones gets first photographer's job in London

September 23, 1951—King George VI's left lung removed

January 31, 1952—Princess Elizabeth and Prince Philip leave for Australasian tour

February 6, 1952 — James MacDonald, valet to King George VI, discovers king dead in his bed at Sandringham when he brings in tea at 7:30 A.M.

February 15, 1952 — King George VI buried at Windsor

March 24, 1952 — Death of Queen Mary

May 5, 1952 — Elizabeth and Philip move into Buckingham Palace; Princess Margaret and the Queen Mother move into Clarence House

December 19, 1952 — Peter Townsend is granted a divorce

June 2, 1953 — Coronation of Queen Elizabeth II

August 21, 1955 — Princess Margaret informs the Queen Mother that she is determined to marry Peter Townsend

October, 1955 — Peter Townsend arrives in London from Belgium, meets with Princess Margaret and the Queen Mother

October 31, 1955 — Princess Margaret makes official announcement that she has decided not to marry Group Captain Peter Townsend

February, 1957 — Princess Margaret and Antony Armstrong-Jones dine together at Elizabeth Cavendish's party in Chelsea

February 19, 1960 — Birth of Prince Andrew

February 26, 1960—Engagement announced between Princess Margaret and Antony Armstrong-Jones

May 6, 1960—Princess Margaret marries Antony Armstrong-Jones

November 3, 1961—Birth of Viscount Linley of Nymans

May 1, 1964—Birth of Lady Sarah Armstrong-Jones

December 18, 1967—Princess Margaret, Lord Snowdon, Queen Elizabeth II, Prince Philip and the Queen Mother meet at Buckingham Palace to discuss the possibility of a divorce between Margaret and her husband

February, 1976—*News of the World* prints photographs of Princess Margaret with Roddy Llewellyn in Mustique

March 17, 1976—London *Daily Express* announces that Princess Margaret and Lord Snowdon are separating

March 19, 1976—Kensington Palace sends out official announcement of Princess Margaret and Lord Snowdon's separation

1977—Peter Townsend's book, detailing his life with King George VI and the royal family, is published

1977-1978—Princess Margaret joins the rest of the royal family in a full slate of duties commemorating Queen Elizabeth's Silver Jubilee